The Cake Club

Also by Susie Quick

Quick Simple Food

Go Bananas! 150 Recipes for America's Most Versatile Fruit

The Cake Club

DELICIOUS DESSERTS AND STORIES FROM
A SOUTHERN CHILDHOOD

Susie Quick

ST. MARTIN'S GRIFFIN ☙ NEW YORK

www.stmartins.com

Book design by Michelle McMillian

Library of Congress Cataloging-in-Publication Data

Quick, Susan
    The cake club: delicious desserts and stories from a southern childhood / Susie Quick—
1st ed.
        p. cm.
    Includes index.
    ISBN 0-312-24374-X
    1. Cake. 2. Desserts. I. Title
TX771.Q35 2004
641.8'653—dc22   2003058769

First Edition: February 2004

10   9   8   7   6   5   4   3   2   1

The ladies were cool and fragile in pastel prints: most of them were heavily powdered but unrouged; the only lipstick in the room was Tangee Natural. Cutex natural sparkled on their fingernails, but some of the younger ladies wore Rose. They smelled heavenly. I sat quietly, having conquered my hands by tightly gripping the arm of the chair, and waited for someone to speak to me.

Miss Maudie's gold bridgework twinkled. "You're mighty dressed up, Miss Jean Louise," she said. "Where are your britches today?"

"Under my dress."

—HARPER LEE, *To Kill a Mockingbird*

Contents

· ·

Acknowledgments

. . . .

This cookbook is composed of the recipe cards and jotted notes of my mother, as well as those of my aunts, cousins, great-aunts, and grandmothers: the late Ora Mae Lanham Akers, the late Genevieve Akers, the late Martha Lucas Burford, Anita and Doris Lee Gandee, the late Opal Akers Hicks, Sherri Gandee Moore, the late Julia Lucas Paterson, the late Venora Akers Wallace, and the late Nellie Teresa Lucas Williamson. I apologize for any inadvertent plagiarism for recipes that may have come from other books and magazines that have been unknowingly co-opted by one of the contributors.

In addition I've included recipes contributed by the members of the Cake Club, and this book is dedicated to them: Mildred Baldwin, Daisy Stemple Bennett, Marge Ferrell, Dorothy Fowler, Ruby Harris, Marian Helmick, Reva Johnson, Kathryn Kessell, Barbara Kosa, Betty Lawrence, Betty Long, Brenda Long, Carolyn Miller, Coralie "Corky" Miller, Elaine Sampson, Isabel Schuman, Jean Stover, Louise Smith, June Thompson, and my mother, Emma Mae Williamson.

I'm happy, too, to include recipes from members of my own Cake Club of sorts, the friends with whom I have enjoyed many laughs, the best and worst of times, and copious amounts of great food. I call them Women Who Rock. Members past and present include: Toni Allocca, Rebecca Bothwell, Bonnie Buckner, Anne Brown, Linda Combs, Kerri Conan, Kathy Dukas, Karin Eaton, Sean Ehlers, Jill Forbert, Germaine Johnson, Sarah Belk King, Carol Kramer, Lori Longbotham, Roxanne Martin, Ouita Michel, Barbara Moutenot, the late Minnie Pearl, Susie Wolfe Query, Lisa Rutledge, Loreli Schellist, Kathy Snyder, Donna and Patti "Cakes" Tauscher, Abigail Walch, Kay Shaw West, Grace Whitney, and Susan Wyland.

These are their stories and their fabulous recipes.

Introduction

·······························

Whenever life's lessons serve me more than I can chew, I head for the kitchen. Once, when I was having premarital misgivings, I spent the entire weekend one-on-one with the oven making Julia Child's recipe for French baguettes. It's a bit of a blur now, though I do remember some aggressive dough kneading, which explains the end results: though pretty to look at the baguettes were inedible, as dense and stiff as tomato stakes (and just as tasty). But the effort was worth what I got out of it. Exorcising my marriage fears made me focus my thinking so that by Monday morning I'd formed a plan to:

A. inform the groom in the least offensive way possible and return the ring ("*Really,* it's *me,* not you. . . .");
B. return the silver, china, fondue set, and caviar ice bowls to about two hundred would-be well-wishers; and,
C. transform thirteen sky blue taffeta bridesmaid dresses into throw pillows.

This type of stress relief is genetic. Like a needlepointed homily nearly all the women in my family seem to subscribe to the belief, "When in doubt, *cook!*" My mother, Emma, copes with holiday anxiety by creating an all-you-can-eat sugar buffet of hand-dipped chocolates, fifty dozen cookies, and at least ten layer cakes and pies. Because, as only my mom can reason, "Not everyone is a chocolate person!" You see, to my mother food *is* love—God bless her—and she is a woman who simply loves *way too much.* After Christmas dinner, for instance, when the extended family is sprawled about the living room lazily rubbing their bellies and sighing at how full they are, she cheerily carries a tray of homemade fudge about the room, oblivious to the hand motions waving her away—*sorry, all full!* She continues in Donna Reed–fashion, even offering up the forbidden sweets to the diabetics in the crowd. "Why, a little can't hurt!" is another of Emma's homilies. Oh, but it does indeed hurt when you're already stuffed to the gills, and my sister and I stay on orange alert in case someone lapses into an insulin-induced coma.

For years I fought the urge to become too much like my domestic-goddess mother, nervous energy simmering as she baked her way through one family crisis after another. The relaxing part for her, I think now, was sitting down at the dinner table and watching as we hungrily shoveled in her latest creation, only occasionally remembering to tell her how delicious it was before dashing out the door.

After I got over the idea that spending time in the kitchen and being a feminist weren't mutually

My mother, Emma, famous for flouting the law.

exclusive, I began to embrace my culinary leanings, and cooking became my refuge from a hectic life of deadlines and must-have meetings. Occasionally, like Emma, I'll find myself pounding away at a chicken breast the way someone might throw a ball against a wall. But more often, making a pie or just being in the kitchen leafing through a cookbook while it bubbles in the oven is the way I forget about my to-do list for a while. Instead of taking a yoga class or getting a massage like my friends, I engage in some old-fashioned cooking therapy.

I think I inherited this obsession for cooking through the DNA of the women in my family—my mother, grandmothers, and aunts on both sides. For them, preparing a meal was much more than a chore; it was their means of expression, and they got a great deal of satisfaction from doing it well. Most of their everyday cooking was pretty simple—smothered pork chops, fried chicken, and lots of side dishes, corn bread, and biscuits. But desserts were something special, the place where a cook could really flex her muscles.

My mother was no different: she used sugar and butter the way an artist might use paint, to create beautifully decorated cakes and other baked delicacies. You see, Emma never needed to know if someone was coming for she was always baking a cake! She still bakes incessantly, in fact. I've watched her wrap up a couple of her brown sugar pound cakes, tuck them beneath her arm, and head out the door with her cocker spaniel, Luther, for a walk in the neighborhood. She'll return an hour or so later, minus the cakes and some worry.

I've come to realize that for my mother, dessert is a way to celebrate her life, transcending the lack of so many comforts she dreamed about as a young girl growing up in the Depression years in Appalachia. She was creating confections she could only glimpse in the windows of the bakeries in Charleston, but never afford to buy.

Although Emma has accumulated a wealth of recipes, they were always written on note cards or scraps of paper and scattered about her cookbooks, tucked between pages of some of her favorites. I've been after her for years to gather them together but she never seemed to find the time. Not long ago, though, she sent me a large envelope and there they were: dozens of recipes of her favorite cakes, pies, and cookies. She included the family collection as well—wonderful handwritten, yellowed cards. Something she'd meant to do for years, the note said. "It might even make a book!" Well, I had to agree, and that's what began this very project.

Among the recipes were a number of favorites from Emma's friends who were members of the Cake Club, as it was called. This was a group of housewives, friends, and neighbors who shared a love of food and camaraderie. The club met once a month for an informal cake-decorating class and luncheon. Since we had the largest living room the members gathered at our house, each bringing a plain frosted cake to decorate, a card table to work on, and a covered dish to share. Although the women were enthusiastic about the hobby, the real purpose of the get-together was to let their hair down and have some fun, which was pretty rare for this crew—especially for my mother, who approached housework and motherhood with the earnestness of a Presbyterian minister. All that changed on club day, and my sister, Linda, and I got to see another side of Emma, a woman who was shy, funny, and artistic. To prepare for the class she would practice replicating flowers from her garden with icing, down to the subtle hues of a hybrid rose and the fuzzy stamen of an iris. It had to be perfect for club day, and when the other ladies approved she beamed with pride.

Bonding with the ladies was empowering for my mother and all the members of the club. I think it gave them the confidence and courage—and humor—to deal with the challenges so many of them faced in those years before the women's movement really took hold.

This book collects recipes and a few quirky stories, but it is also about appreciating the sweetness of life (because it ain't always a honey of a time), and remembering relatives and friends through the tasty dishes they made. Like Emma, I have relied on my women friends through many phases of my life, from marriage at a too-young age, numerous career moves, and several relationships, to the realization of writing my own books and living in the middle of horse country in Kentucky. Life is definitely sweeter than it has been in some time. And it's a helluva lot more fun celebrating it with your friends and a nice piece of cake.

Put all my friends in a room and I think you will see common denominators. In addition to a recipe for a good blender cocktail, they possess a twinkle of wit, a penchant for dancing on tables, and a generosity of spirit that is rare and true. We may not talk as much as we'd like but we never fail to connect with what made us friends in the first place— food. Each of the recipes is my small way of paying tribute to my sisters, and I hope you will enjoy their recipes and stories too.

The Cake Club will now come to order . . .

The Cake Club

Cakes from the Club

Funeral Cake
   (Coconut–Sour Cream Layer Cake)

Coconut Filling and Frosting

Powdered Sugar Pound Cake

Different Poppy Seed Cakes

Orange Glaze

Brown Sugar Pound Cake

Penuche Frosting

Twenty-Minute Sponge Cake

Caramel Glaze

Butter Layer Cake

Lemon Whipped Cream Frosting

Opal's Date-Nut Applesauce Cake

Oatmeal Pan Cake with Broiled Pecan-
   Coconut Topping

Sister Nell's Prune Spice Cake

Brown Sugar Frosting with Walnuts

Kay's Carrot Cake with Pineapple and
   Coconut

Cream Cheese Frosting

Yellow Cupcakes

Peanut Better and Jelly Frosting

Cream-Filled Chocolate Cupcakes

Fudge Icing

Chocolate Chip–Coffee Chiffon Cake

Coffee Frosting

Chocolate Buttermilk Layer Cake

Dark Chocolate–Orange Frosting

Mother-in-Law Cake

Mocha Buttercream Frosting

Kid-Friendly Mother-Approved
   Coca-Cola Sheet Cake

Coca-Cola–Chocolate Frosting

Tunnel of Love Chocolate-Macaroon
   Bundt Cake

Aunt Martha's Hickory Nut Cake

The Cake Club's White Fruitcake

Meet the Cake Club

Once a month my mother's Cake Club met at our house. Their official name was the Fancy Frosters Cake Club, but that got shortened early on. Club day was one filled with sticky icing, gooey gossip, and (best of all) food.

I loved both eavesdropping on the women and devouring the lunch for it was a potluck of great repute. My sister and I would often vie to see who could lay claim on being sick first, so we could miss school on club day. Since I had the more licentious nature, I usually beat her to the punch and became an expert at plotting mysterious ailments that always managed to convince my mother that the world would be a lot safer with me at home, in bed. Since it couldn't be anything gastrointestinal (which would preclude me from eating), I had to be creative. There were dramatic fainting spells but these had to be rationed to remain effective. My true Joan Fontaine moment involved falling out of bed while appearing to be asleep.

(Note: This particular stunt takes some preparation, so plan ahead.) Here's how it's done: tuck all the sheets and blankets neatly under the mattress. Then slither your body inside the cocoon. Begin to angle yourself forty-five degrees so that you slowly slide out of bed—headfirst—while still keeping the rest of your body inside the bedclothes. The important thing is to make it look real. Once you're in place, close your eyes and wait. What will likely happen is your mother will enter and be immediatcly appalled to see her darling child with her head on the hard floor and sinuses draining the wrong way for God knows how long. She kneels and gently shakes you (usually there is concern in her voice). You "awake" moaning at the horrid headache you undoubtedly have. (Once, this actually happened and my nose bled like a headless chicken so it was a precedent I took advantage of many times until it lost its shock value.)

But back to the club and more importantly, lunch. The thing that made club day food so special was that it was not the normal everyday fare, by which I mean beef stew, meat loaf, mashed potatoes, pork chops and gravy, etc., etc. This was *Lady* Food, all delicate and precious, arranged on pretty plates and just begging to be eaten. There was fresh parsley in the recipes rather than dried, and radish roses and carrot curls accessorized the platters.

The buffet generally consisted of casseroles and congealed salads that slithered from Jell-O molds just before serving. Finger sandwiches with the crusts trimmed and freshly brewed iced tea with mint leaves were not uncommon. Hot canapés emerged from our oven, which had never happened before. It was party time at our house and it wasn't even a holiday. My mother brought out her best tablecloth and napkins for the occasion, linens my brothers had never even seen, let alone rested their elbows upon. And a cut-glass punch bowl with glasses that I didn't even know we owned. Lunching with the ladies this way was my first real brush with elegance and it made me feel years older.

Best of all, there were desserts. It was like the Pillsbury Bake-Off (in more ways than one), only better because everything was made from scratch. Beneath their sweet exteriors the cake clubbers were stone cold competitors, my mom included. That's probably why everything was its ultimate best. I still remember the peach dumplings my mom's friend, Reva J., brought one day, still bubbling hot from the oven. It's one of the best things I have eaten *ever*. Pies were a favorite and the crusts were blue-ribbon worthy, never frozen.

On the surface it was all about decorating cakes but what my mother and her friends did not acknowledge was that the Cake Club was a de facto *women's group* (it was the feminist era, after all). So as one of the women served as instructor, the rest of the members would pump icing flowers and scrollwork on their cakes and share child-rearing tips, compare the annoying habits of their spouses, and address any current events that deserved commentary. Most of them were pretty liberal in their belief that women were superior in all the important ways, and that the key to a successful marriage was managing your husband well. None of them had a particularly easy life—no country club memberships or trips to the salon for a pedicure for these home-makers. One theme was common: that husbands were good for some things (fixing appliances), but hopeless at others (any kind of cooking, helping with the children, and generally gabbing about life).

It could get rowdy at times. Elaine was the first woman I knew who openly dyed her hair and was nicknamed the sexpot. One day she showed off her new push-up leopardskin bra in my presence. It was inspiring—the first I had ever seen and a far cry from Emma's tame white Cross Your Heart. Elaine cracked her gum and painted her toenails coral to match her lipstick, all of

This is the G-rated version of Emma's famous bikini cake that she would happily adapt to suit a man's taste.

which seemed to team perfectly with the animal-print lingerie.

The women were a little less bawdy than they might otherwise have been due to the presence of Betty, a Nazarene who always wore a tight bun and long-sleeved dresses, (the lengths of which were closer to the ankle than the knee) even in the heat of August. Schooled in the classic Wilton method, Betty strolled about the room correcting everyone's form on puffs and scrollwork, the subtleties of multi-petaled daffodils and roses, and so forth as they progressed toward more advanced artistry like fondant and marzipan fruits.

I loved all the ladies but my very favorite was Mildred who, simply put, knew how to laugh at herself and at life (which was not so common if you grew up in Appalachia). Mildred was "a real color TV" my mom would say, and she shared her foibles and predicaments to entertain the girls. A classic story of hers involved a hunting trip she and her husband took in the early years of their marriage. They hiked to the top of a wooded hill where Mildred found a sunny rock to lie on and read while her husband went off in hot pursuit of squirrel. Mildred had a long pony-tail at the time. Somehow her husband had gotten turned around in the woods and didn't real-ize he had circled back. He spotted Mildred's "tail," assumed it was a squirrel, took aim, and grazed her face with buckshot. When he ran up and saw what he'd done he fainted dead away. Mildred hoisted her husband over her shoulder and carried him off the hill to drive them both to the doctor. She still has some of the buckshot in her neck, she likes to point out as proof, for it was too close to an artery to remove.

Another time a man came to Mildred's door about a piano she had advertised for sale. It was Jay Rockefeller (*the* Jay Rockefeller), the governor at the time. She was in the kitchen washing dishes when she answered the door, not bothering to dry her hands on a kitchen towel. He had a trooper with him and she thought perhaps there was a problem with her taxes. When he told her that he was there about the piano she took his hand and nearly shook it off, saying, "Well, put her there, Governor—dishwater and all!" She invited him in and made him a fried bologna sandwich, which he ate with gusto at her kitchen table. He bought the piano.

Cakes from the Club

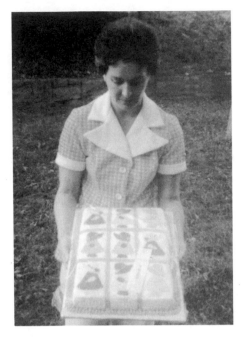

A serious competitor, Emma takes the prize for a quilt-themed cake at the county fair.

My mother—"the Virgo" as the ladies would often point out—was a lean, mean baking machine, and with the practice she received at the club her technique soon reached perfection, which was the goal. Emma went on to teach the craft herself as well as making and selling all sorts of novelty cakes for the community (once she even did a replica of a semi truck that brought the truck company owner to tears). Her specialty was a "bikini cake" in the shape of a woman's torso wearing a pink polka-dot bikini, which she would happily customize if the customer wanted it, even making it topless, or as in one instance I recall, bottomless. She also did beautiful, multitiered wedding cakes, especially for everyone in the family. Our home was always filled with the aroma of cakes baking in the oven. The dining room and kitchen were an obstacle course of cake layers and icing flowers drying on parchment-lined trays.

Emma sometimes entered her cakes at the county fair. My favorite picture of my mom was taken after she won a blue ribbon for one of her exuberantly decorated creations. She is dressed in a blue-and-white gingham pantsuit holding her cake up for the photographer. With her dark curly hair cut in layers and her high cheekbones, she could be Loretta Lynn's sister.

For me the Cake Club revealed the mysteries of womanhood. The house became a different place when it was filled with the laughter and perfume of all the ladies. Family gatherings weren't nearly as much fun and they usually just meant more work with all the cleaning and cooking beforehand and the cleanup afterward. It was rare for the women where I grew up to simply get together for a neighborly visit. They were usually too busy doing housework or tending a garden. Nearly all of them had a house full of children and a few held part-time jobs to help make ends meet. A club meeting with a hobby attached was probably an acceptable excuse in those days and more palatable to their husbands who might have to forgo a home-cooked supper on club day.

The ladies saw each other through a lifetime of ups and downs, illnesses, and death, bound together as they were by butter and sugar, and real friendship. They have remained friends for years and still are, though a few are now in heaven, hopefully eating cake.

The Cake Club

Funeral Cake

(COCONUT–SOUR CREAM LAYER CAKE)

This is my mother, Emma's, specialty—a supermoist chilled coconut cake she makes for holidays and other special occasions. It is also the cake she alway takes to a home after a death in the family, which is why my sister and I call it funeral cake. *You need to start one or two days ahead because both the filling and the frosted cake need to stand for the flavors to fully develop. It starts with a white cake mix. I know what you're thinking—yuck. But I've tried it with a scratch cake and it's not nearly as good. Emma prefers Duncan Hines. I also tried substituting whipped cream for the Cool Whip my mom uses and it was also a failure. So stick with Emma on this and you'll have a really nice cake to show for it.*

1 box white cake mix (preferably Duncan Hines)

Coconut Filling and Frosting (recipe follows)

Preheat oven to 350°F. Butter two 9-inch round cake pans and line bottoms with waxed or parchment paper.

Make and bake the cake according to package directions. Transfer to racks and cool 5 minutes. Invert onto racks to cool completely.

Follow directions for filling and frosting.

Makes one 9-inch 4-layer cake
Serves 12 to 16

Coconut Filling and Frosting

1 cup sour cream

1½ cups confectioners' sugar

3 (6-ounce) packages frozen shredded
    coconut, thawed

1 (8-ounce) container frozen non-dairy
    whipped topping, thawed

Fold together the sour cream, sugar, and 2 packages of the coconut in a large bowl. Cover with plastic wrap and refrigerate overnight. Reserve 1 cup of coconut mixture.

To fill and frost cake: Slice cakes in half horizontally to make 4 layers. Place one layer on a plate. Place one-third of coconut mixture on top. Repeat with remaining layers.

Fold the reserved coconut mixture into the whipped topping. Frost sides and top of cake. Sprinkle top and sides with remaining package of coconut. Refrigerate cake 4 hours or overnight. Before serving, allow the cake to sit 20 minutes at room temperature. Keep leftovers refrigerated.

Makes about 2 cups filling or 3 cups frosting

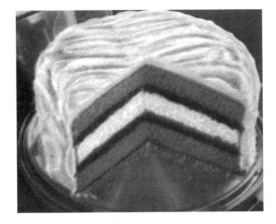

Powdered Sugar Pound Cake

My maternal great-grandmother, Ora Mae Akers, baked her pound cakes in a coal stove. It was she who taught my mother the secrets of cake baking. Ora knew exactly how much heat to build up in the stove (coal burns very hot) and how long it would take for a pound cake to bake in the ring-shaped iron pan. (All the baking pans then were iron as it could best distribute the fluctuating heat of coal or wood fires.) Her cakes probably could not be replicated with today's ingredients; they were made with fresh butter and buttermilk from the family's dairy, and homegrown eggs.

This pound cake is a lighter version with a very fine texture. My mother often makes it when I visit, and it's one of my favorites, especially as a base for peach or strawberry shortcake.

1 cup (2 sticks) unsalted butter, softened	6 large eggs
1 (1-pound) box confectioners' sugar, sifted (plus additional for sprinkling over cake)	3 cups cake flour (not self-rising)
	¼ teaspoon salt
	⅓ cup milk
	1½ teaspoons vanilla extract

Preheat oven to 350°F. Butter and flour a 10-inch Bundt or tube pan.

Place the butter in a large mixing bowl with sugar. Beat with an electric mixer on medium speed 5 minutes until light and creamy. Add the eggs, one at a time, beating for 1 minute after each addition. Scrape sides and beaters and beat in vanilla.

Stir together the flour and salt. Add the dry ingredients to the butter mixture, a third at a time, alternately with the milk. Beat on lowest speed just until blended. Scrape batter into prepared pan.

Bake 50 minutes to 1 hour, or until a long wooden skewer inserted in the center comes out clean and edges are slightly pulled away from sides. Cool in pan on a rack 10 minutes. Remove from pan and continue to cool on rack. Sprinkle with confectioners' sugar before serving.

Makes two 9 × 5 × 3-inch loaf cakes or one 10-inch Bundt cake
Serves 12 to 16

Different Poppy Seed Cakes

This is Emma's name for a pound cake that's not only different but delicious. Here's what she says about it:

I've been baking cakes for almost sixty years and this is one of my favorites. It's a large, moist cake that turns out right every time. Soaking the poppy seeds overnight makes them tender. It's best if you make it the day before serving.

3 tablespoons poppy seeds	2 cups sugar
²⁄₃ cup buttermilk	5 large eggs
2½ cups cake flour (not self-rising)	1 tablespoon grated orange zest
½ teaspoon baking powder	1 teaspoon vanilla extract
¼ teaspoon salt	1 teaspoon almond extract
1 cup (2 sticks) unsalted butter, softened	Orange Glaze (recipe follows)

Stir together the poppy seeds and buttermilk in a small bowl. Cover with plastic wrap and refrigerate overnight. Preheat oven to 325°F. Butter and flour 10 mini Bundts or one 10-inch Bundt pan. Sift flour, baking powder, and salt into a medium bowl. Using an electric mixer, beat sugar and butter in a large bowl until light and fluffy. Add the eggs 1 at a time, beating well after each addition. Beat in zest and extracts. With mixer on lowest speed, beat in dry ingredients alternately with buttermilk–poppy seed mixture.

Pour batter into prepared pan or pans. Bake until tops are brown and tester comes out clean, about 20 to 25 minutes for mini Bundts or 60 to 70 minutes for the large pan. Transfer pans to rack. Cool cakes 10 minutes. Loosen sides of pans with a butter knife. Turn cakes out onto wire cooling racks. When barely warm, drizzle with glaze.

Makes 10 mini Bundts or one 10-inch Bundt cake
Serves 12 to 16

Orange Glaze

½ cup fresh orange juice
1 teaspoon almond extract

½ cup confectioners' sugar

Whisk together all ingredients in a small saucepan and bring to a boil. Drizzle or brush on warm cakes.

Makes about ²/₃ cup glaze

That afternoon was like the center of the cake that Berenice had baked last Monday, a cake which failed. . . . Frankie had been glad the cake had failed, not out of spite, but because she loved these fallen cakes the best. She enjoyed the damp, gummy richness near the center, and did not understand why grown people thought such cakes a failure. It was a loaf cake, that last Monday, with the edges risen and light and high and the middle moist and altogether fallen—after the bright high morning the afternoon was as dense and solid as the center of that cake.

—Carson McCullers, *The Member of the Wedding*

Brown Sugar Pound Cake

If you like the taste of waffles, you will love this maple-flavored pound cake. The majority of fans of my mother's signature cake prefer the complete package with the frosting but I like it plain. Emma says:

Every time we have a get-together my friends ask if I'm serving this cake. A little maple flavoring makes the difference, and the icing tops it off. I've been baking this cake for years and when we have bake sales, my friends always recognize the cake and snatch it up.

2½ cups bleached all-purpose flour

1 teaspoon baking powder

½ teaspoon salt

1¼ cups (2½ sticks) unsalted butter, softened

1 cup packed light brown sugar

1 cup granulated sugar

5 large eggs

½ cup milk

1 teaspoon vanilla extract

1 teaspoon maple flavoring

Penuche Frosting (recipe follows), optional

Preheat oven to 350°F. Butter and flour a 9 × 5 × 3-inch loaf pan or a 10-inch Bundt pan. Sift together the flour, baking powder, and salt. Cream the butter and sugars with an electric mixer for 5 minutes until light and creamy. Add eggs, one at a time, scraping and beating well after each addition. Combine the milk and flavorings. Add flour and milk alternately to the creamed butter until just blended. Scrape into prepared pan. Bake about 60 minutes (in the Bundt pan), or 70 minutes in the loaf pan, until a wooden skewer inserted in the center comes out clean.

Cool in pan on rack 15 minutes. Turn out onto rack to cool completely.

Makes one 9 × 5 × 3-inch loaf cake or one 10-inch Bundt cake
Serves 12 to 16

Penuche Frosting

½ cup (1 stick) unsalted butter

1 cup packed light brown sugar

2 tablespoons light corn syrup

⅓ cup milk

½ teaspoon vanilla extract

½ teaspoon maple flavoring

3 cups confectioners' sugar

Combine butter, brown sugar, corn syrup, milk, and flavoring in a medium saucepan and bring to a boil, stirring to blend. Remove from heat and stir in confectioners' sugar. Beat until smooth and cool until barely warm. Frost cakes while frosting is barely warm.

Makes about 2 cups frosting

Twenty-Minute Sponge Cake

This is the easiest little snack cake you can stir together in under 30 minutes. Served warm or at room temperature, it's perfect for a picnic or potluck. Before serving, make the warm caramel glaze and pour it over the cake in the pan.

1 cup cake flour	2 large eggs
1 teaspoon baking powder	1 cup sugar
¼ teaspoon salt	1 teaspoon vanilla extract
2 tablespoons unsalted butter	Caramel Glaze (recipe follows)
½ cup milk	

Preheat oven to 375°F. Sift together flour, baking powder, and salt; set aside. Butter a 9-inch square pan.

Warm the butter and milk in a small saucepan over low heat until butter melts. Keep warm.

In a large bowl beat the eggs and sugar with an electric mixer on medium speed for 2 minutes. Reduce speed to low and add dry ingredients and vanilla, scraping the bowl well. Slowly add the warm milk mixture until just blended. Scrape batter into prepared pan.

Bake 20 minutes, until top springs back when lightly touched with fingertips. Cool in pan on rack. When cool (or barely warm), top with caramel glaze. Cut into 9 squares and serve.

Makes one 9-inch square cake
Serves 6 to 9

Caramel Glaze

½ cup light brown sugar   1 tablespoon unsalted butter

¾ cup heavy cream   pinch of salt

Place glaze ingredients in a medium saucepan over moderate heat. Stir with a wooden spoon and bring to a simmer. Simmer 7 minutes, stirring frequently, until glaze is thickened. Cool until barely warm. Pour over cake.

Makes about 1 cup glaze

Butter Layer Cake

This is a classic yellow layer cake filled with lemon curd and raspberry jam—just the thing to serve for tea. It has a whipped-cream frosting so you will need to refrigerate the cake both before and after serving. Purchased lemon curd tastes closer to homemade if you add a little fresh juice and zest. Look for a brand with all-natural ingredients.

2½ cups cake flour (not self-rising)
1¼ teaspoons baking powder
½ teaspoon salt
1 stick plus 4 tablespoons unsalted
   butter, softened
1½ cups sugar
3 large eggs
¾ cup milk

1½ teaspoons vanilla extract
¼ cup lemon curd mixed with
   1 teaspoon lemon juice and
   1 teaspoon finely grated lemon zest
⅓ cup seedless raspberry jam
Lemon Whipped Cream Frosting
   (recipe follows)

Preheat oven to 350°F. Butter and flour three 8-inch cake pans; set aside. Sift together flour, baking powder, and salt; set aside.

Beat butter and sugar with an electric mixer 5 minutes until light and fluffy. Add eggs one at a time, scraping and beating well after each addition.

Combine milk and vanilla. With the mixer at lowest speed add dry ingredients to the creamed butter alternately with milk mixture in three parts, scraping and beating until ingredients are just blended. Scrape the batter into prepared pans, spreading to edges.

Place the cake pans on 2 oven racks so that one pan is not directly over another. Bake 20 to 25 minutes until a wooden skewer inserted in the center comes out clean. Cool cakes on racks 10 minutes. Invert cake layers onto racks, then turn right side up to cool completely.

To assemble: Save the prettiest layer for the top. Place one layer on a serving plate. Top with lemon curd, spreading to within 1 inch of cake edge. Top with another cake layer and spread with jam in the same way. Place the third layer on top and press lightly into place.

Spread a thin layer of frosting on the top cake layer. Refrigerate the cake 1 hour. Frost the sides and top of the cake with remaining frosting. Refrigerate until ready to serve, at least 1 hour. Allow the cake to stand at room temperature 20 minutes before serving. (This cake will also freeze well, if wrapped tightly in Saran Wrap.)

Makes one 8-inch 3-layer cake
Serves 16

Lemon Whipped Cream Frosting

A microplane grater is the best tool for making fine zest.

1½ cups heavy cream

1½ teaspoons finely grated lemon zest

⅓ cup purchased lemon curd mixed
with 1 teaspoon fresh lemon juice

In a medium bowl, whip the cream with an electric beater until soft peaks form. Fold in the zest and curd by hand. Keep chilled until ready to use.

Makes about 3 cups frosting

A house is beautiful not because of its walls,
but because of its cakes.

—Old Russian Proverb

Opal's Date-Nut Applesauce Cake

Not *The Grapes of Wrath,* but the Akers clan (my mother's side of the family), who farmed the old-fashioned way, with blood, sweat, and tears. From left: William Jarret Akers and two of his children, Lester and Opal.

My maternal grandmother Opal (Ma Ma) rarely applied a glaze, let alone frosting, to her cakes since she preferred them plain and simple. I always loved her applesauce cake best for its subtle spice and dense moistness. But when I revisited the recipe it seemed overly sweet and left an oil slick in the palm of my hand. Since Opal's heyday we've learned a lot about using applesauce as a fat replacer. I fiddled with her recipe, which originally called for an entire cup of oil and two cups of sugar. It's now much lighter in texture and just sweet enough. Ma Ma always used black walnuts, a strong-tasting nut that is more readily available in the fall. I've substituted English walnuts instead. Dusting the raisins and dates with flour keeps them from sinking to the bottom of the cake pan.

1/3 cup canola oil

1 cup granulated sugar

2 large eggs

2 cups all-purpose flour

1/2 teaspoon baking soda

1 teaspoon baking powder

1/2 teaspoon salt

1 teaspoon ground cinnamon

1/2 teaspoon ground allspice

1/2 teaspoon freshly grated nutmeg

1/4 teaspoon ground cloves

1 1/2 cups applesauce

3/4 cup chopped golden raisins,
   dredged in flour

3/4 cup chopped dates, dredged in flour

1/2 cup chopped pecans

1/2 cup chopped English walnuts
   (or black walnuts)

confectioners' sugar for dusting

Preheat oven to 350°F. Butter and flour a 10-inch Bundt pan.

In a large mixing bowl, cream together the oil, sugar, and the eggs. In another bowl, stir together the flour, salt, baking soda, cinnamon, nutmeg, and cloves. Add to the creamed mixture along with the applesauce, raisins, dates, and nuts and mix until batter is well blended. Pour into prepared pan.

Bake 45 to 50 minutes, or until a toothpick inserted in the center comes out clean. Remove from oven and cool in pan 10 minutes. Turn onto a rack to cool completely. Before serving, transfer to a plate and lightly dust with confectioners' sugar.

Makes one 10-inch Bundt cake
Serves 12 to 16

*To order black walnuts by the pound, contact Hammons Products Company, 888-495-5688; or order online at www.black-walnuts.com.

Oatmeal Pan Cake

WITH BROILED PECAN-COCONUT TOPPING

I remember my mother making this snack cake all the time for my father, who never had much of a sweet tooth but enjoys this enormously. It is moist, chewy, and wholesome tasting. If you wish, you can scatter some chocolate chips on top before broiling it, though I prefer the gooey coconut and butterscotch flavors alone.

1¼ cups boiling water

1 cup old-fashioned rolled oats

1¾ cups bleached all-purpose flour

1 teaspoon ground cinnamon

1 teaspoon baking soda

½ teaspoon salt

½ cup (1 stick) unsalted butter, softened

1 cup packed light brown sugar

3 large eggs, beaten

1 teaspoon vanilla extract

Topping:

4 tablespoons unsalted butter

¾ cup packed light brown sugar

3 tablespoons half-and-half or whole milk

1 cup chopped pecans

1 cup flaked coconut

Preheat oven to 350°F. Butter a 9 × 13 × 2-inch pan. Combine the boiling water and oats in a small bowl; set aside to cool.

Sift together the flour, cinnamon, baking soda, and salt. Combine the butter and brown sugar in a large bowl and beat with an electric mixer 5 minutes, until creamy. Beat in eggs and vanilla. Beat in the oatmeal until thoroughly blended. With mixer on lowest speed gradually add flour mixture to bowl. Transfer to prepared pan and bake 40 to 45 minutes, until a toothpick inserted in the center comes out clean.

To make topping: While cake bakes, melt butter in a small saucepan. Stir in the remaining topping ingredients and set aside.

When the cake is done, remove from oven and preheat the broiler. Arrange a rack about 4 inches from broiler. Gently spread the topping across the cake. Place beneath broiler; watching carefully, broil 1 to 2 minutes, until it turns lightly golden brown. Cool cake in pan on a wire rack. Cut into squares. The cake is good served a little warm or at room temperature.

Makes one 9 × 13 × 2-inch cake
Serves 12 to 16

Sister Nell's Prune Spice Cake

Nellie Teresa Lucas

My father's mother was Nellie Teresa Lucas Williamson, though most in the family called her Sister Nell. She died when my father was only six, and we heard many stories about her when we were growing up. She loved partying and dancing and played the ukulele. There are a few telling photos of her dressed as a flapper, stepping off a train or draped across the hood of a Packard. Sister Nell became an imaginary friend to my sister and me, and we never failed to set a place for her at our tea table. I loved it when my great-aunt Martha (her sister) would tell me how much I was like her (especially when I was being mischievous).

This is her recipe for an old-fashioned prune cake. It is very moist, dense, and rich. The cardamom might seem like an affectation, but I tried it because I was out of allspice and liked the results even more. A microplane grater (the one that looks like a rasp) is the best for grating the zest from the lemon. If you don't have one, use the smallest holes on a box grater, then tap the grater on a cutting board to release the zest. The cake is also good without the frosting, and drizzled with a glaze or dusted with confectioners' sugar.

2 cups pitted prunes, quartered

2¼ cups bleached all-purpose flour

2 teaspoons ground cinnamon

¾ teaspoon freshly grated nutmeg

¾ teaspoon ground cardamom or
   allspice

½ teaspoon baking powder

1 teaspoon baking soda

½ teaspoon salt

1 cup (2 sticks) unsalted butter

1¼ cups sugar

2 teaspoons finely grated lemon zest

2 teaspoons vanilla extract

3 large eggs

1 cup sour cream

Brown Sugar Frosting (recipe follows),
   optional

Preheat oven to 350°F. Butter and flour a 10-inch springform pan or a 10-inch Bundt pan and set aside.

Sift together the flour, cinnamon, nutmeg, cardamom, baking powder, baking soda, and salt. Combine the butter, sugar, zest, and vanilla in a large bowl and beat with an electric mixer on medium speed 5 minutes, until light and fluffy. Add the eggs, one at a time, beating and scraping well after each addition. On the lowest speed, add the dry ingredients alternately with the sour cream, beginning and ending with the flour. Don't overmix.

Fold the prunes in by hand. Scrape the batter into the prepared pan and spread batter to edges. Bake 50 to 55 minutes (or a bit longer in a springform pan), until a wooden skewer inserted in the center comes out clean.

Cool the cake in the pan on a wire rack 10 minutes. Run the tip of a knife around the edges of the cake to loosen it. Remove the sides of the pan (or invert the Bundt pan onto the rack when it's nearly room temperature). Sprinkle with confectioners' sugar while still warm. Cool to room temperature and slice into wedges. Alternately, frost sides and top when cake is barely warm with Brown Sugar Frosting.

Makes one 10-inch springform cake, or a 10-inch Bundt cake
Serves 12 to 16

Brown Sugar Frosting with Walnuts

1 cup packed dark brown sugar

4 tablespoons unsalted butter, softened

¼ cup heavy cream

1 teaspoon vanilla extract

pinch of salt

1 ½ cups confectioners' sugar

½ cup chapped walnuts, lightly toasted

Place the brown sugar, butter, and cream in a medium saucepan and bring to a boil. Cook 2 minutes, stirring, until the sugar is dissolved and the frosting bubbles to the top. Remove from heat and stir in the vanilla and salt. With an electric mixer on medium speed, add 1 cup of the confectioners' sugar and beat to incorporate. Gradually add the remaining sugar, beating until the frosting is smooth and creamy. Immediately spread the frosting over the cake while it is still warm. If the frosting starts to dry or becomes crusty, return it to low heat and stir just until it becomes creamy again.

This makes enough to frost a 9¹/₂-inch round cake or a 10-inch Bundt cake.

Kay's Carrot Cake with Pineapple and Coconut

When I was first a struggling freelance writer (not to be confused with the current situation), I baked carrot cakes on the side for a small café in Nashville. At my peak I turned out five or six a day in my little cottage kitchen. They were monstrous: four thick layers with 4 cups of grated carrots (more like a carrot cake "tower"), 4 cups of cream cheese frosting, and weighing at least as many pounds. The cakes were a hit and I worked and slaved producing them, honing it to a science until one day I figured out I was making about two bucks each for hours and hours of work. I moved to New York soon afterward and the café owner begged me to sell her the recipe. This is not the exact recipe (baker's secret), but a more deluxe version from my Nashville friend Kay West that is spicy and hefty with carrots. The key to this extra-moist cake is pulsing the fruit and grated carrots together in a food processor before adding it to the batter.

2¼ cups all-purpose flour

2 teaspoons baking powder

2 teaspoons baking soda

½ teaspoon salt

1 tablespoon ground cinnamon

1 teaspoon freshly grated nutmeg

1 teaspoon ground allspice

1 medium Granny Smith apple, peeled, cored, and chopped (about 1 cup)

½ cup drained crushed pineapple in unsweetened juice

3 cups grated carrots (about 6 medium carrots)

4 large eggs

1 cup packed dark brown sugar

¾ cup granulated sugar

1 cup canola oil

1½ teaspoons vanilla extract

⅔ cup flaked coconut

½ cup chopped pecans or walnuts

Cream Cheese Frosting (recipe follows)

Preheat oven to 350°F. Butter a 10-inch Bundt pan or 9 × 13 × 2-inch pan. Sift together the first seven dry ingredients (through allspice), and set aside.

Place the apple, pineapple, and carrots in the bowl of a food processor and pulse about 5 times to combine (but don't liquefy them). Set aside.

Combine the eggs, sugars, oil, and vanilla in a large bowl and beat with an electric mixer until well blended. Add the carrot mixture and stir to combine. With mixer on lowest speed, gradually add the flour mixture until just incorporated. Fold in the coconut and nuts. Pour batter into prepared pan.

Bake 50 to 60 minutes, until the edges of cake have pulled away from sides of the pan and a wooden skewer inserted in the center comes out clean. Transfer to a rack and let the cake cool in the pan to nearly room temperature. Run the tip of a butter knife around edges of pan to loosen it, then place a plate over the bottom and invert.

Frost and refrigerate until ready to serve. Serve cold or at room temperature.

Makes one 10-inch Bundt or 9 × 13 × 2-inch cake
Serves 12 to 16

Cream Cheese Frosting

8 ounces cream cheese, softened

5 tablespoons unsalted butter, softened

1 teaspoon vanilla extract

1½ cups confectioners' sugar

Combine all ingredients in a large bowl and beat with an electric mixer until smooth.

Makes about 2 cups frosting

Frozen Cake and Its Implications

Aunt Nora was not well. Again. And it was us who had brought it to light. Now the phone lines were buzzing with talk of doctors and homes and who knows what else.

We'd struck out that morning on our Stingrays, pedaling wildly on the concrete streets of our cousins' neighborhood. Wind in our hair, cheeks flushed, tears streaking back to our ears. The four of us raced away like giddy puppies sprung from their pen. We smiled to each other as plans were hatched, pushing the established boundaries and exploring places we weren't supposed to go. Like across the railroad tracks and down to the river. My cousins were seldom allowed such freedom—it was only when their naughty kin from the country came for an overnight that the rules got bent. After our visit, any subsequent smart-aleck comments and acts of willfulness were no doubt attributed to our influence.

After a couple of hours of our tour de suburbia, past grade school playgrounds, favorite teachers' houses, and forbidden shanties next to the tracks, we grew tired and thirsty. It came to us that our aunt Venora's house was just up the road and we had only to pedal some ten minutes to a lonely widow's bungalow filled, we were certain, with unimaginable treats like short bottles of Coca-Cola, potato chips, and Butterfingers.

We rationalized our unannounced visit by the fact that Aunt Norie (which is what we children called her) was alone since her husband had died several months before and, after all, wasn't it just the proper thing to do for us all to pay her a visit, say howdy and sit a spell? But when we rode up to the house the curtains were drawn and a long wooden ladder was resting on the chain-link fence angled from the driveway up to the kitchen windowsill. It looked peculiar but we supposed someone was just doing some work on the house.

Venora Akers in happier days. She was the youngest and prettiest of my mother's aunts.

"We should go," said Cousin Sherri, the eldest and wisest.

"Oh, no, I'm sure it's fine," the enabler in me said.

So we knocked. After peeking from behind a curtain Aunt Norie opened the door, blinking at the daylight streaming into her smoke-filled living room.

"Well," she said. "This *is* a surprise!"

Aunt Norie wore a faded blue floral housedress and her darkly dyed hair was sticking up like a shrub. She wore no makeup and without penciling in, you could see faint scars that cut through her eyebrows, the result of a car accident in her youth. Her soft, flushed cheeks were as dimpled as bread dough. She lit a Winston and sat at the kitchen table, the air squishing out from the vinyl cushion.

"Would you girls like some pop?"

We nodded sheepishly, thinking our fantasies were about to come true. She told us to help ourselves. There were two bottles of Double Cola opened in the fridge, both partially drunk. Hearts sank at the off-brand soda. Still, we grabbed them, not wanting to appear ungracious. We divvied it up in the coffee cups she pointed to on the dish rack and sat at the table, drinking the flat soda without a word.

"How about some cake?" she said. We brightened. Cake would more than make up for flat cheap pop.

She parked the Winston in a heavy glass ashtray and walked to the freezer to withdraw a store-bought chocolate cake with white frosting. Sara Lee. Then Aunt Norie pulled a large carving knife from the drawer. Our eyes grew big, but instead of killing us she used it to cut the cake into four giant hunks and placed it on a plate she sat in the middle of the table. She handed us each a fork;

"Don't be shy—*eat!*" It sounded like an order.

We picked up our forks and jabbed into the cake but it was solid as clay.

"Aunt Norie, it's too froze!" said Cousin Sherri.

"Well, give it some time, then," she said, shrugging and picking up her cigarette.

The Cake Club

And so we sat and chipped away at our cake while Aunt Nora stared absently out the window.

I finally piped up: "Aunt Norie, why do you have the ladder leaning on the house like that?" I was side-kicked and elbowed at the same time.

"Well, I'll tell you why," she said, turning her eyes on me and stabbing out the Winston. "Someone's put a charge in the fence and every time I touch it I get shocked. So I climb through the window when I need to go out and come in. Wood don't shock you none—don't you know that?"

"Um, no ma'am," I said, ashamed of myself. Poor Aunt Norie had come undone and we all knew it.

We shoveled in what remained of the freezer-burned cake and said our good-byes. We pedaled home slowly, not knowing what to do about the circumstances. On the one hand, we probably shouldn't have gone there unannounced—or at all, Sherri added. Their mother, Aunt Doris, would be none too pleased by this news. On the other hand, there was the moral imperative of informing the adults about the fence and the chance that our elderly aunt straddling a rickety ladder would break her neck.

I was right. Once we told the story, not a word was said about our straying out of territory, and wheels began to turn. Aunt Doris immediately called our mother.

When I was older I learned Venora's story, which is incredibly sad. After an automobile accident and a number of other emotional setbacks, she fell into a cloud of depression that lasted into adulthood. In her older years she was subdued but pleasant. From her quiet demeanor you'd never know all she'd been through.

Yellow Cupcakes

I made these for my friend Toni's children's birthday parties and they were a huge hit with both kids and adults. They're really adorable with the little jelly dimple in the center.

¾ cup (1½ sticks) unsalted butter, softened

1½ cups granulated sugar

3 large eggs

2 cups all-purpose flour

1 teaspoon baking powder

1 teaspoon baking soda

1 cup buttermilk

1½ teaspoons vanilla extract

Peanut Butter and Jelly Frosting (recipe follows)

Set the rack at the middle of the oven and preheat the oven to 350°F. Line two ½-cup-size muffin tins with paper liners.

Beat the butter and sugar in a large mixing bowl with an electric mixer for 5 minutes at medium speed until light and fluffy. Beat in eggs, one at a time. Scrape the bowl and beaters and beat well.

Sift the flour with the baking powder and baking soda. Add a quarter of the flour mixture to the butter-egg mixture, then add a third of the buttermilk. Repeat, beginning and ending with the flour mixture and scraping well after each addition.

Divide batter evenly among muffin tins. Bake the cupcakes 15 to 18 minutes, until a toothpick inserted in the center comes out clean. Cool in pan on a rack 2 minutes. Then turn cupcakes out on the rack to cool completely before frosting.

Makes 2 dozen cupcakes

Peanut Butter and Jelly Frosting

Don't use natural-style peanut butter in this recipe (the type with the oil on top) as the consistency will not be as smooth.

½ cup creamy peanut butter
2 tablespoons unsalted butter, softened
3 tablespoons heavy cream

2 cups confectioners' sugar (sifted if lumpy)
¼ cup grape jelly

In a large bowl of an electric mixer, beat the peanut butter and butter, until blended. Add the cream and sugar and beat until smooth. (Makes about 2 cups frosting). Frost cupcakes. With your fingertip, scoop out a small amount of the frosting from the center of each cake.

Place the jelly in a glass dish and heat in the microwave oven approximately 30 seconds until softened. Place about ½ teaspoon of jelly in the center of each cupcake.

Makes about 1 ¼ cups frosting

Cream-Filled Chocolate Cupcakes

My mother always made these very special cupcakes for my birthday parties, though with the luscious creamy filling it's a dessert grown-ups will love too. I changed the filling somewhat—adding marshmallow cream—to make it a bit lighter. There are three parts to the recipe, so it takes a little time to make, but it's definitely worth the trouble. Make the cream filling first and freeze it while you make the batter. While the cupcakes are baking, make the icing.

Cream filling:

2 (3-ounce) packages cream cheese, softened

1/3 cup marshmallow cream

1 large egg

2 tablespoons granulated sugar

1/2 teaspoon vanilla extract

1/2 cup semisweet mini chocolate chips

Cupcake batter:

1 1/2 cups all-purpose flour

1 cup granulated sugar

1/2 cup unsweetened cocoa powder, preferably Dutch process

1 teaspoon baking soda

1/2 teaspoon salt

3/4 plus 2 tablespoons water

1/3 cup canola oil

2 teaspoons cider vinegar or distilled white vinegar

1 1/2 teaspoons vanilla extract

Fudge Icing (recipe follows)

Make filling: In a medium bowl with an electric mixer, beat cream cheese, marshmallow cream, egg, sugar, and vanilla for about 1 minute or until mixture is light and fluffy. Fold in chocolate chips. Place filling in freezer while you prepare cupcake batter (or refrigerate for 1 hour or longer).

Make cupcakes: Preheat oven to 350°F. Line the cups of a 12-cup muffin tin with paper or foil baking cups.

In a large bowl, combine the flour, sugar, cocoa, baking soda, and salt, stirring with a whisk to break up any lumps. In another bowl, combine the water, oil, vinegar, and vanilla. Gradually add the liquid ingredients to the flour mixture, whisking until completely blended.

Place a tablespoon of batter in the bottom of each muffin cup. Then place a dollop of chilled cream filling (about 1 tablespoon) into each cup (you'll have some filling left over). Fill cups about three-quarters full with remaining cupcake batter. Bake 25 to 28 minutes, or until the cupcakes are slightly crusty around the edges. Cool in muffin tins 15 minutes. Gently lift cupcakes out of pan and place on a wire rack to cool completely. Then frost with fudge icing as directed.

Makes 12 cupcakes

Here's what's cookin'
Recipe from:

1 Baked 9 inch
1 1/4 cups suga
6 T. corn stare
2 C. water
4/3 c lemon
3 egg yolk
1 1/2 t lemon
2 t vinegar
3 T Butter
Mix sugar
together in top
boiler.

Here's what's cookin' CRANBERRY CAKE   Serves ____
Recipe from the kitchen of DORIS GANDEE

2-1/4 cups flour
1 cup sugar
1/4 tsp. salt
1 tsp. soda
1 tsp. baking powder
1/2 cup chopped nuts
1 cup diced dates
1-1/2 cups cranberries
Place in large mixing bowl —
don't mix with mixer — Add & mix

Fudge Icing

This fudgy icing coats cupcakes nicely and dries to a glossy finish.

⅓ cup heavy cream
⅔ cup semisweet mini chocolate
  chips, or 4 ounces coarsely chopped
  semisweet chocolate

Place the chocolate in a small mixing bowl. In a small saucepan bring cream to a boil and pour over chocolate. Stir with a whisk until chocolate melts completely and icing is smooth and creamy. Cool to room temperature.

When cupcakes are completely cool dip the tops, one by one, into the icing. Return cupcakes to wire rack and let icing set until it's no longer sticky.

Makes about 1 cup

Chocolate Chip–Coffee Chiffon Cake

My friend Susan Wyland is married to a cardiologist and is one of the most health-conscious people I know about her diet—no meat, steamed fish, lots of vegetables, and nary a drop of fat. Her eating habits are a paradigm of virtue—except when it comes to dessert! I'm sure this is why we're able to go out to dinner and remain good friends. This is a story of her favorite cake. One taste and you'll understand why. Here's Susan's note that came with the recipe:

"This was my favorite birthday cake as a little girl; I requested it year after year. It was so big, so tall, and so impressive, and I loved the coffee/chocolate flavor combination and the deliciously sticky frosting. In my twenties, I asked my mother for the recipe, and she gave it to me. The first time I made it, I knew how much she loved me—this cake is no small amount of work, but definitely worth it."

2¼ cups cake flour (not self-rising)
3 teaspoons baking powder
½ teaspoon salt
1½ cups superfine, granulated sugar
½ cup canola oil
5 large egg yolks
¾ cup cold, strong coffee
1 teaspoon vanilla extract

3 ounces chilled semisweet chocolate, shaved (Mom used Baker's)
1 cup egg whites, at room temperature (approximately 7 or 8 from large eggs)
½ teaspoon cream of tartar
Coffee Frosting (recipe follows)

Preheat oven to 325°F.

Sift the flour, baking powder, salt, and sugar together three times. Make a well and add, without stirring, the oil, unbeaten egg yolks, coffee, and vanilla. Stir the liquids with a whisk, then slowly stir in the flour. Whisk until the batter is smooth. Stir in the shaved chocolate.

Place the egg whites in a large bowl with the cream of tartar. Beat with an electric mixer until very stiff (but not dry). Add the flour mixture, ¼ at a time, folding after each addition until combined. Scrape into an ungreased 10-inch tube pan with a removable bottom. Bake 1 hour and 15 minutes, until a wooden skewer inserted in the center comes out clean.

Immediately upon removing from the oven, hang the cake upside down over an empty wine bottle, slipping the center over the bottle's neck (weird, I know, but it keeps the cake from collapsing). Allow it to hang there until completely cool. Remove from pan and place upright on a plate. Frost the top and sides with Coffee Frosting.

Makes one 10-inch tube cake
Serves 12 to 16

> There was a big cake and two little ones on Miss Maudie's kitchen table. There should have been three little ones. It was not like Miss Maudie to forget Dill, and we must have shown it. But we understood when she cut from the big cake and gave the slice to Jem. As we ate, we sensed that this was Miss Maudie's way of saying that as far as she was concerned, nothing had changed. . . Suddenly she spoke: "Don't fret Jem. Things are never as bad as they seem."
>
> —Harper Lee, *To Kill a Mockingbird*

Coffee Frosting

1 large egg white

1 cup lightly packed brown sugar

¼ cup cold, strong coffee

1 teaspoon vanilla extract

½ teaspoon baking powder

Place egg white, brown sugar, and coffee into a medium metal bowl placed over a pan of barely simmering water. Beat with an electric mixer for 7 minutes, until thick and fluffy. Remove from heat and beat in vanilla and baking powder until incorporated. Immediately frost the cooled cake with the frosting.

Makes about 2 cups frosting

Chocolate Buttermilk Layer Cake

This is a tall and moist chocolate layer cake anyone will love. The texture is dense, just like a classic chocolate layer cake should be. The orange adds a nice touch to the dark, rich frosting.

¾ cup (1½ sticks) unsalted butter, softened

1½ cups sugar

3 large eggs

1 teaspoon vanilla extract

2 cups cake flour (not self-rising)

⅔ cup unsweetened cocoa

2 teaspoons baking soda

½ teaspoon salt

1 cup plus 2 tablespoons buttermilk

Dark Chocolate–Orange Frosting (recipe follows)

Preheat oven to 350°F. Butter two 8-inch round baking pans. Line bottoms with waxed or parchment paper; butter the paper.

Combine the butter and sugar in a large bowl and beat until light and creamy, about 3 minutes. Add eggs, one at a time, beating well after each addition and scraping sides and beaters.

Sift together the flour, cocoa, baking soda, salt, and baking powder. Stir together the vanilla and buttermilk and add alternately with flour mixture to the butter mixture; beat until blended. Divide batter among the prepared pans and smooth the tops.

Bake 25 to 30 minutes or until a wooden skewer inserted in center comes out clean. Transfer to racks and cool 10 minutes. Invert cakes onto racks to cool completely.

To assemble cake: Place 1 cake layer on a plate. Spread ⅓ of frosting over cake. Top with second layer; spread remaining frosting over top and sides of cake. Allow the cake to stand 2 hours before serving. (Can be prepared 1 day ahead. Cover and refrigerate. Bring to room temperature before serving.)

Makes one 2-layer 8-inch cake
Serves 12

Dark Chocolate-Orange Frosting

1 cup heavy whipping cream

½ cup (1 stick) unsalted butter, cut into 1-inch pieces

⅓ cup sugar

¼ cup water

¼ teaspoon salt

16 ounces good-quality semisweet chocolate, finely chopped

2 teaspoons finely grated orange zest

1 tablespoon orange liqueur such as Cointreau or Grand Marnier

Combine the first 5 ingredients (through salt) in a large saucepan over medium heat and bring to a simmer, whisking until butter melts and sugar dissolves. Remove from heat. Add the chocolate and whisk until smooth. Whisk in the zest and liqueur. Scrape the frosting into a large bowl and cool, stirring occasionally, until thick enough to spread, about 1 hour.

Makes 3 cups frosting

Mother-in-Law Cake

I collect old recipe brochures and my favorite is a tattered one titled "The Calendar of Cakes, Fillings and Frostings," published by Swans Down Cake Flour in the 1930s. The "calendar" contained 365 different cakes—one for each day of the year—with recipes for birthday cakes, holidays, and anniversaries (both silver and golden). It has a recipe for a spice cake that seems to be the ancestor of this one, which is adapted from a reader's recipe sent to Gourmet magazine in the 1960s. It has to be the spiciest spice cake around (no, the tablespoon each of ground cinnamon and cloves is not a mistake) and it's my very favorite layer cake of all. The flavor combination of the intense spices and mocha frosting is just brilliant. Make sure your spices are fresh and pungent; if not, purchase new bottles so the cake will taste its very best. I make it in stacked square layers for birthdays but be sure to hide a piece to enjoy later. There won't be any leftovers.

2 cups cake flour (not self-rising)	1 cup (2 sticks) unsalted butter, softened
2 tablespoons unsweetened cocoa	
1 tablespoon ground cloves	1½ cups sugar
1 tablespoon ground cinnamon	4 large eggs
1 teaspoon freshly grated nutmeg	2 teaspoons vanilla extract
1½ teaspoons baking soda	1¼ cups buttermilk
1½ teaspoons baking powder	Mocha Buttercream Frosting
½ teaspoon salt	(recipe follows)

Preheat oven to 350°F. Butter the bottom and sides of two 8 × 2-inch square cake pans or two 9 × 2-inch round pans.

Spoon the flour into dry measuring cups and level off with a knife. In a medium bowl sift together the flour and next 7 ingredients (through salt); set aside.

In a large bowl with an electric mixer beat together the butter and sugar until light and fluffy, about 5 minutes. Add the eggs, one at a time, beating well after each addition. Beat in the vanilla.

Begin adding the flour in 3 parts, alternately with the buttermilk, scraping and beating after each addition until just combined. Divide the batter between the pans, smoothing the top with a spatula. Bake in the middle of the oven, 25 to 30 minutes, or until a wooden skewer comes out clean.

Cool cake layers in pans on racks 5 minutes. Invert on racks and cool completely before frosting.

Makes one 8-inch square, or 9-inch round 2-layer cake
Serves 12 to 16

Mocha Buttercream Frosting

3 ounces unsweetened chocolate,
  chopped
3 cups confectioners' sugar, sifted
¼ cup very strong coffee

½ cup (1 stick) unsalted butter,
  softened
pinch of salt
2 teaspoons vanilla extract

In a metal bowl set over a pan of barely simmering water melt chocolate, stirring until smooth. (Alternately, melt the chocolate in a glass bowl in the microwave for 1 minute on high.) Let the chocolate cool slightly while you cream the other ingredients.

In a bowl with an electric mixer, beat the confectioners' sugar and coffee until smooth. Add the melted chocolate and beat well. Cool to room temperature. Beat in the butter, salt, and vanilla. Add more sifted confectioners' sugar, if necessary, to make frosting more spreadable.

To assemble cake: Place one cake layer on a serving plate and spread with about ½ cup of frosting. Top with other layer. Frost the sides and then the top of the cake, making decorative swirls on top.

Makes about 2 cups frosting

Kid-Friendly Mother-Approved Coca-Cola Sheet Cake

I've tasted lots of recipes for this Southern favorite over the years but I think my mom's version is the best. The milk chocolate sheet cake is simple to make—just stir everything together in a large bowl with a wooden spoon—so it's an ideal recipe to make with a child. Emma keeps the cake in the pan (hers has a plastic top), which makes it easy to take to a picnic or potluck. Some recipes call for the addition of 1½ cups of miniature marshmallows to the batter, so that's up to you.

2 cups all-purpose flour

2 cups sugar

1 teaspoon baking soda

1 cup (2 sticks) unsalted butter

¼ cup unsweetened cocoa powder

1 cup Coca-Cola

½ cup buttermilk

2 large eggs, beaten

1 teaspoon vanilla extract

Coca-Cola–Chocolate Frosting
  (recipe follows)

Preheat oven to 350°F. Butter a 9 × 13 × 2-inch baking pan. Stir together the flour, sugar, and baking soda in a large mixing bowl; set aside.

Place the butter, cocoa, and cola in a medium saucepan and bring to a boil. Remove from heat and stir into dry ingredients. Stir in the buttermilk, eggs, and vanilla. Pour into prepared pan.

Bake 30 to 35 minutes until a toothpick inserted in the center comes out clean. Cool 20 minutes and spread with frosting while still warm and sprinkle with nuts, if using.

Makes one 9 × 13 × 2-inch cake
Serves 12

Coca-Cola-Chocolate Frosting

½ cup (1 stick) unsalted butter

3 tablespoons unsweetened cocoa powder

6 tablespoons Coca-Cola

3½ cups (about one 1-pound box) confectioners' sugar

1 cup coarsely chopped pecans, toasted (optional)

Combine the butter, cocoa, and cola in a medium saucepan and bring to a boil. Remove from heat and stir in sugar until smooth. Immediately spread over a warm cake. Sprinkle cake with nuts, if desired.

Tunnel of Love Chocolate-Macaroon Bundt Cake

I met fellow food writer Kerri Conan on a press trip and we became fast friends as she was just one of the wittiest and smartest people I have ever met. She married and moved to a small town in Kansas a few years ago, but we stay in touch via e-mail and on the phone supporting each other's freelance lifestyle. Most of the time, we talk about recipes as we both are usually working on a book while juggling magazine assignments. Among other things, we share a fondness for the defunct Jell-O 1-2-3 triple-layered gelatin desserts in shades of pink. But another passion was the even fancier coconut-filled chocolate Bundt cake that came in a box. My hat is off to Kerri for re-creating it from scratch. Not too surprisingly, it's a whole lot better than the original. Here's Kerri's story and recipe:

Around 1970 when Pillsbury introduced the mix for Chocolate Macaroon Bundt Cake, my family spent a week at my grandparents' apartment outside of New Orleans. We made extra batches to take along on our endless visitations with relations. Everyone marveled at how the coconut filling didn't get mixed up with the devil's food cake. I was just ten, but somehow perfectly content to watch *Match Game* on TV, play canasta with a bunch of old ladies, and monitor the ash on my mama's cigarette, which she always let burn too long between flicks. I must have been high on this cake. Making it now from scratch is pretty easy and guaranteed to wow the crowd around a card table.

For the cake:

6 ounces semisweet chocolate morsels

¼ cup unsweetened cocoa

¼ cup milk

2½ cups all-purpose flour

2 teaspoons baking powder

½ teaspoon salt

1 cup unsweetened shredded coconut

2¼ cups granulated sugar

1 cup (2 sticks) unsalted butter, softened

6 large eggs

1 teaspoon vanilla extract

2½ cups confectioners' sugar   1 teaspoon vanilla extract

¼ cup evaporated milk

Preheat oven to 350°F. Lightly butter and flour a 10-inch Bundt pan.

In a small saucepan over low heat, combine chocolate, cocoa, and milk, stirring constantly until everything is melted and dissolved. Set aside. In a medium bowl, sift together flour, baking powder, and salt. In another small bowl toss coconut with ¼ cup of the sugar.

With an electric mixer, cream the butter until fluffy. Gradually add remaining sugar. Beat on medium speed until light, about 3 minutes. With mixer running on lowest speed add eggs, one at a time, beating well between each addition. Add vanilla.

Remove one cup of batter and stir into the coconut mixture until just incorporated. Add the melted chocolate to the remaining cake batter and mix until blended.

Pour a little less than half of the chocolate batter into the prepared pan and smooth the top. Drop small spoonfuls of the coconut batter around the middle of the cake, and gently spread to create a ring of filling (be careful not to touch the sides of the pan). Now top the whole thing with the remaining chocolate batter. It should completely cover the filling.

Bake in center of preheated oven for about an hour, until a toothpick inserted in the center comes out clean. Let rest in the pan on a wire rack until completely cool. Invert onto a cake plate.

Combine glaze ingredients and whisk until smooth. (Add a little more milk if it's too thick.) Drizzle on top of the cake and let it set before slicing.

Makes one 10-inch Bundt cake
Serves 12 to 16

Aunt Martha's Nut Cake

My aunt Martha only made one cake and this is it. I love its flavors—hickory nuts, butter, and sugar, the flavors of fall. It's pretty difficult to find hickory nuts; pecans or hazelnuts can be used as well. This simple, light-textured cake is quite good eaten plain but even more delightful served with some sweetened whipped cream and sliced oranges (or very ripe persimmons if you have them).

1 cup (2 sticks) unsalted butter
1½ cups packed light brown sugar
1 teaspoon vanilla extract
3 large eggs
2 cups all-purpose flour
2 teaspoons baking powder
¼ teaspoon salt

¾ cup milk
1 cup finely chopped hickory nuts*, pecans, or hazelnuts
1 cup heavy cream
2 to 4 tablespoons sifted confectioners' sugar

Preheat oven to 325°F. Butter and flour one 9 × 5 × 3-inch loaf pan.

Place the butter, sugar, and vanilla in a large bowl and beat with an electric mixer 5 minutes until light and fluffy. Beat the eggs in, one at a time, scraping and beating well. Sift together the flour, baking powder, and salt. Add alternately in 3 parts with the milk, scraping and beating between additions. Fold the nuts in by hand.

Scrape batter into the prepared pan. Bake 50 to 60 minutes, or until a wooden skewer inserted in the center comes out clean. Cool in pan 10 minutes before inverting on a rack to cool completely.

Meanwhile, whip the cream and confectioners' sugar to taste until stiff. Before serving, dust the cake with confectioners' sugar and slice. Serve with whipped cream on the side.

Makes one 9 × 5 × 3-inch loaf cake

*To order hickory nuts, call Wolfie's Nuts at 888-889-6887, or order online at www.wolfiesnuts.com.

The Cake Club's White Fruitcake

....

While I've tolerated most of the fruit cakes I've been served, this is the only one I have ever enjoyed. Truthfully, as a genre I can't stand them—how they smell, the way they look. But this fruitcake is lovely. I first sampled it at one of the Cake Club's lunches and it is white and delicate with pretty colors and a texture closer to pound cake. It tastes and looks just like a holiday. There are quite a few ingredients but it's pretty simple to make (for a fruitcake, that is). Although it is rich enough without dousing it with alcohol, I do like a touch of pear brandy or white rum for the extra kick. It keeps for ages wrapped tightly in the fridge. Slice it very thinly and serve with a small dollop of sweet, whipped cream with a dash of liquor in it.

1½ cups (3 sticks) unsalted butter, softened

2 cups sugar

2 teaspoons vanilla extract

1 teaspoon almond extract

2 to 3 teaspoons grated orange zest (from 1 orange)

4 cups cake flour (not self-rising)

2 teaspoons baking powder

½ teaspoon salt

2 cups golden raisins

2 cups candied (or dried) cherries

2 cups candied (or dried) pineapple, finely chopped

8 ounces flaked sweetened coconut

2 cups coarsely chopped slivered almonds or pecans

1 cup milk

1½ cups egg whites (from about 1 dozen large eggs), room temperature

Preheat oven to 325°F. Butter a 10-inch tube pan (or angel food cake pan) with a removable bottom and line bottom with parchment or waxed paper. Butter paper and dust inside of pan with flour, shaking out excess.

In a large bowl with an electric mixer, cream the butter and sugar until light and fluffy, about 5 minutes. Beat in extracts and zest.

Sift together the flour, baking powder, and salt. Toss with the next 5 ingredients (through almonds). Add the flour mixture alternately to the butter mixture with the milk, beating well after each addition.

In another bowl, beat the egg whites on high speed until stiff peaks form. Fold into batter until just incorporated. Scrape into prepared pan. Bake 70 to 80 minutes, or until a wooden skewer inserted in center of cake comes out clean. Cool in pan until warm. Sprinkle with a few tablespoons of brandy or rum, if desired. Remove from pan when completely cool and discard paper. Wrapped tightly in plastic and foil, the cake will keep in an airtight tin about 2 weeks (or longer, refrigerated). (If you want to make it up ahead of time, it freezes up to a month.)

Makes one 10-inch tubecake
Serves 12 to 16

I am sending your Christmas herewith, a white fruitcake . . . I have never understood why everybody loves it but they swear they do . . .

—Reynolds Price, Kate Vaiden

All Kinds of Pies

Aunt Genny's Sour Cherry Crumble Pie

Bonnie's Favorite Shaker Lemon Pie

Brown Sugar Apple Pie

Deep-Dish Peach Pie

June's Cider Vinegar Piecrust

Extra-Tart Apple Crisp

Half-moon Apple Pies

Peach-Raspberry Half-moon Pies

Reva J.'s Peach Dumplings

Lemon Meringue Pie

Butter Piecrust

The Best Chocolate Cream Pie

Coconut-Banana Cream Pie

Flaky Piecrust for a Single
   Deep-Dish Pie

Minnie Pearl's Chess Pie

Butternut Squash Pie

Frozen Peanut Butter Pie

Graham Cracker–Nut Crust

Frozen Caramel (Dulce de Leche) Pie

All Kinds of Pies

When it came to pies, I was a late bloomer. While young Martha Stewart was selling cherry pies and peach tarts to the neighbors before her first training bra, my recipe for success was all about exerting the least amount of effort for pay. My first financial foray was painted rocks. I spent days adorning them with psychedelic colors and then loaded my faux gems in my brother's Radio Flyer and hauled them door-to-door. Sometimes I'd get a nickel for one, sometimes a dime. If I looked particularly pitiful, I could squeeze a quarter out of an old feller.

Just like Martha's home in Nutley, New Jersey, we too had a garden and orchard in our backyard. Instead of dutifully gathering up the apples and peaches for making pie and jam (as did Miss Martha), my siblings and I pelted each other with them. Green fruit inflicted the most damage, especially when aimed at the head. Emma didn't seem to mind as long as no one cried, since our trees—despite the lack of pruning—were usually loaded with fruit. My favorite apples for eating were the golden russets, and once they turned a burnished gold, I ate them until my stomach hurt. Emma made fabulous pies and applesauce with them.

Although some people might think of elaborate layer cakes as the height of Southern desserts, I'll always think of pies. If you happen by a little café in Charleston you might notice on the chalkboard, following the day's specials, a lengthy list of pies that far outnumbers anything else on the menu. I didn't attempt them actually, until I moved to New York City and you were hard pressed to find anything as simple as a homemade peach pie (though there were fancy tarts galore).

There were always plenty of pies at our family gatherings. Every summer my aunt Martha's Primitive Baptist church held their annual retreat or "association" on her farm, and

Even at a tender age, I could eat a pie this big.

the array of food was vast and wonderful. An entire table would be devoted solely to all the cakes and pies (which I suppose, were not considered sinful by the pious crowd). You can't imagine what splendor this seemed to a child peering at them from eye level. Following are some of these recipes from old family recipe cards and newspaper clippings, as well as a few versions of my own.

Aunt Genny's Sour Cherry Crumble Pie

Aunt Genevieve was sexy. She walked down the street in high heels, a smart hat, swinging her purse to keep time to her step. When she got older, she dyed her hair black and wore bright red lipstick and nail polish. On holidays she arrived with bushels of presents and baked delicacies, drank beer, and pulled out her false teeth and made them clack for the children, which was her improvisation of a ventriloquist act. We loved Genny—she was a riot. Sadly, we lost our favorite aunt, and much laughter, early on.

For years she cooked at The Grille, a galley-size diner next to The Virginian movie theater in Charleston. She was a helluva short-order cook and worked the counter for tips as well. Her specialty desserts were cherry tarts, which you can make with this recipe if you wish. This pie is simple and delightful. Sour cherries are best, but if you can't find them, sweet ones will do. If using the latter, reduce the sugar to 1/2 cup.

1 9-inch single Flaky Piecrust
   (recipe page 80)
6 cups pitted, fresh sour cherries
   (about 2½ to 3 pints)
1 cup granulated sugar

2½ tablespoons quick-cooking tapioca
1 tablespoon kirsch (cherry brandy),
   optional
pinch of salt

Crumble topping:

¾ cup old-fashioned rolled oats
½ cup all-purpose flour
½ cup packed light brown sugar
⅓ cup sliced almonds

½ teaspoon ground cinnamon
pinch of salt
½ cup (1 stick) cold unsalted butter,
   cut into small pieces

Prepare the piecrust as directed for a 10-inch pie and refrigerate while you prepare the remaining ingredients.

Aunt Genevieve was known for her cherry pies and sexy appeal.

Preheat oven to 425°F. Place the cherries in a large mixing bowl and toss with the sugar, tapioca, kirsch, and salt. Pile the fruit into the dough-lined pie plate.

To make crumble topping: In a food processor (or in a bowl using your fingers), combine the oats, flour, brown sugar, almonds, cinnamon, salt, and butter. If using a food processor, pulse until the mixture is the size of small peas. Scatter the topping evenly over the cherries.

Bake the pie 30 to 35 minutes until the fruit is bubbling and the topping and crust are just beginning to brown. Reduce the heat to 350°F and continue baking 20 to 25 minutes more, or until the topping is nicely browned. (If crust starts to get overly brown, place a collar of aluminum foil around the edges to prevent further darkening.) Remove from the oven and cool on a rack. Serve warm or at room temperature with vanilla ice cream, if desired.

Makes one 10-inch pie
Serves 6 to 8

Bonnie's Favorite Shaker Lemon Pie

....

(Adapted from The Shaker Cook Book: Not by Bread Alone, *by Caroline B. Piercy, Crown Publishers, 1953.)*

Bonnie Buckner and Anne Brown were my landladies when I lived in Nashville. I was more of an adopted child than a tenant (I had recently been divorced and was in need of some mothering). I always started the day with a visit to Bonnie's kitchen in her antique-littered log house, to fill a mug with coffee and get my first dose of comedy.

"Haaaw-neee, let me tell you!" Bonnie would say. The next thing I knew I was late for work again, but it was always worth it.

Bonnie and I spent many hours "up-ended" as she'd say, working like Amish farm wives in the ever-expanding flower beds on the property, planting clumps of flowers that were mostly begged, borrowed, or stolen. Bonnie taught piano, but she also managed estate sales for a bank in town—a job with hidden perks for us plant lovers. Bonnie and I would load up our shovels and set out on a tour of homes of the recently deceased and take our pick of the peonies and azaleas, which were sure to be discarded when the new owners hired a landscaper. A neighbor once called the police on us, but since Bonnie could talk a leg off a chair I wasn't the least bit worried and kept on digging up a lilac bush as she smoothed things over with the men in blue.

We ate well during the time I lived there, which was a godsend as I was poor from my job as a reporter at a non-unionized newspaper. Usually Bonnie and Anne bought the groceries and I did the cooking.

When she did the estate sales Bonnie always set aside the old cookbooks for me to peruse. My favorite was The Shaker Cook Book: Not by Bread Alone, *by Caroline B. Piercy, which is really a bible of simple cooking, filled with natural remedies, wholesome meals, and homey desserts. Bonnie loved the Shaker lemon pie most of all and I made it often for us. I think of Bonnie every time I make the pie or stop by the side of the road to dig up a wild flower. She would be proud.*

All Kinds of Pies

....

3 medium lemons (preferably organic),
   washed
2 cups sugar

Butter Piecrust (page 76) for a
   9-inch double crust
4 large eggs

You can't imagine how delicious a pie this simple can be. Since the recipe calls for using the rind and all, I suggest buying organic lemons. Either way, start by scrubbing the lemons with a drop of dish soap and a soft brush to remove any coating. A mandoline slicer (plastic versions are available inexpensively at houseware stores) will get the lemons paper-thin, which is what you want. You can use a sharp, heavy knife if you don't have a mandoline. Pick out any seeds and discard. Place slices in a medium glass bowl and cover with sugar and toss. Cover and let stand at room temperature 2 hours (or overnight in the refrigerator).

Make the piecrust and line the pie plate and trim crust as instructed. Refrigerate until ready to bake pie.

Preheat oven to 450°F. Roll out the top crust and have it ready. Beat the eggs well and pour over the lemons, tossing gently. Place the filling into the prepared crust. Place the top crust on pie and crimp edges, making a few vents in the center.

Bake 15 minutes at 450°F. Reduce heat to 375°F and bake 20 minutes longer, until the top crust is golden brown and a knife inserted through the vent into the custard comes out clean. Cool on a rack until room temperature.

Makes one 9-inch pie
Serves 6 to 8

Aunt Myrtle's Three-Hour Apple Pie

My father's mother died when he was six. As his father had to travel for business, he was often left with one of his aunts (one of his mother's three sisters) and they all lavished attention on him. My dad is a great storyteller and he had a wealth of material from his side of the family, which had more than its share of spunky women. I always enjoyed the ones about Aunt Clara who was married to Uncle Dewey, a man famous for going on a tear with a bottle. It made her so mad that one night when he passed out she tied him to the bedposts and whaled on him with a broom. The next day he was black-and-blue and had no memory of the incident (but stayed on the wagon a few months longer than customary). Aunt Myrtle was the best cook of them all. She and Uncle Ed were particularly entertaining, to say the least. Their favorite pastime was to play pranks on each other, and there were some outrageous tales. I asked my dad for his favorite story and this is what he sent me:

My aunt Myrtle married Uncle Ed Turner before the Depression in the late 1920s. He was born on a river-bottom farm north of Charleston. As most boys did during that time Uncle Ed had to quit school to either work the farm or go to the coal mines to survive.

Aunt Myrtle taught piano to anyone who could pay or trade for food. He and Aunt Myrtle met and married and tried to keep the farm going. But when the Depression eventually hit no one could afford to take piano lessons, even for food. Aunt Myrtle decided (you may as well know she wore the pants in the family), that it was time for them to move to town. The couple was able to rent a house with the little money they had between them and try city life in Charleston.

My father, Arthur James "Jim" Williamson, and his mother, Nellie Teresa.

Uncle Ed soon found a job as janitor in a large department store downtown. He walked to work about three miles each way. Times being hard, Uncle Ed began stopping for a drink or two on his way home (probably got thirsty with all that traveling; it's understandable). But instead of walking home, it soon became staggering home, with Uncle Ed drinking up the better part of his paycheck at the pool hall.

One day Aunt Myrtle and her sister, Julia, were visiting and drinking iced tea on the front stoop. Myrtle didn't see Uncle Ed approaching and Julia had just mentioned how nice and neat the place looked since they moved in.

"Ed sure must be handy," Julia observed.

At that moment Aunt Myrtle replied, "Yes, he's good at everything except bringing home any money!"

Julia said, "Well, uh, hello, Ed!"

Aunt Myrtle jumped up and dropped her tea glass. Uncle Ed stood and glared at Myrtle and then walked past her into the house. He did not go to work the following day (and did not take another job again, ever). He told Myrtle if she thought she could do any better that's what she should do.

The next morning Aunt Myrtle paid her nickel to the conductor and took the streetcar to the department store where she told the manager that Uncle Ed would not be coming back to work. Instead, Aunt Myrtle became the alteration lady there and stayed until the owners died and the store closed in the 1950s. During that time Myrtle saved enough money to not only buy the house they were living in but the two-story apartment building behind it, as well as two other houses on the adjoining lots. So she did indeed "do better." And Uncle Ed became the handyman for the properties. They stayed together but it was a never-ending feud. Aunt Myrtle, in the power seat you might say, was never satisfied with Uncle Ed's work ethic and Uncle Ed busied himself "getting even," as he put it.

Aunt Myrtle was a great cook. The house always smelled of soups, stews, and a pot of beans flavored with ham hocks. She was an exceptional baker and her apple pies were quite memorable. I was excited one day to be there when she placed one in the oven and she invited me to stay.

That day Uncle Ed happened to be in getting-even mode. So, after Myrtle exited the kitchen, he walked in and turned the oven off without a word or a wink to me, as I sat at the table doing my homework. About half an hour later Aunt Myrtle opened the oven and sniffed at the pie. She told me it wasn't ready yet and I'd have to wait. Forty-five minutes later she came back and same result. She checked it again thirty minutes later and exited, scratching her head. After she left Uncle Ed returned to the kitchen and relit the oven. Aunt Myrtle never knew why that pie took three hours to bake.

The next time I visited I walked up the street and found Uncle Ed sitting on the porch roof with his arms on his crossed knees and his head hanging down. I yelled up at him and asked what he was doing. About that time Aunt Myrtle came out of the house, the screen door slamming shut behind her.

"I'll tell you what the old fool is doing!" she said, agitated. "I had a new roof put on the house and I knew he'd want to go up there and tramp around so I told him to stay off of it!"

Well, that was all Uncle Ed needed to hear, because that's exactly where he went. Aunt Myrtle proceeded to lock all the windows. He was on the tar roof all afternoon in the July heat. Aunt Myrtle finally opened up a bedroom window at suppertime but Uncle Ed stayed put until she'd gone to bed. It wasn't long before payback time.

On summer afternoons Aunt Myrtle liked to rest upon a daybed on the sleeping porch. It was very pleasant with plenty of shade and fragrant flowers—the ideal place for a nap. Uncle Ed had built latticework to enclose the area. After Myrtle dozed off Uncle Ed got busy. He locked the back porch door, went outside, and stuck the water hose nozzle through the latticework, aiming it square at Myrtle. He turned it on full blast and soaked her fully, her screaming and trying to open the kitchen door. He let her cool off until it was time to eat supper. I always wondered what she fed him that night. . . .

All Kinds of Pies

Brown Sugar Apple Pie

Sadly, we don't have Aunt Myrtle's actual recipe but this is a very good deep-dish apple pie with old-fashioned flavors like brown sugar and vanilla. Thankfully, it only takes about an hour to bake.

June's Cider Vinegar Piecrust
(recipe follows)

10–12 medium apples such as Granny
Smith or golden delicious, peeled
and cored and cut into eighths

1½ teaspoons ground cinnamon

½ teaspoon freshly grated nutmeg

1½ teaspoons vanilla extract

1 cup packed light brown sugar

3 tablespoons all-purpose flour

2 tablespoons unsalted butter

1 large egg yolk

1 tablespoon milk

1 tablespoon brownulated sugar

Preheat oven to 400°F. Position rack in the oven to the lower third. Line a large baking sheet with foil and set aside.

To make the filling, combine all the ingredients except the yolk, milk, and brownulated sugar. Let sit for 5 minutes.

Roll out both discs of the dough on a floured surface to make two 14-inch circles. Carefully lay one of the discs into a 10-inch deep-dish pie plate and trim dough to rim. Spoon the apple mixture into the crust. Dot with butter. With water, rub the rim of the crust and carefully place the second circle on top of the apples. Press the crusts together at the rim; trim the overhang with clean scissors to extend 1 inch. Fold overhang under and crimp edges decoratively with fingers. Make a few steam slits on top of the crust.

Combine the egg yolk and the milk and brush the top of the crust. Sprinkle with brownulated sugar. Place on prepared baking sheet and bake for 50 minutes.

Check after 25 to 30 minutes to see if the top crust is getting too brown; if so, tent it loosely with foil and continue baking for the remaining time. Remove from oven and cool 20 minutes. Serve warm with vanilla ice cream, if desired.

Variation for Deep-Dish Peach Pie

Substitute:

8 peaches, peeled and sliced, for the
apples

use ½ to ¾ cup light brown sugar
(depending on sweetness of
peaches)

½ teaspoon freshly grated nutmeg for
cinnamon

1½ tablespoons cornstarch for the
flour

Assemble and bake as directed for apple pie.

Makes one 10-inch double-crust pie
Serves 8 to 10

June's Cider Vinegar Piecrust

2 cups all-purpose flour

1 tablespoon sugar

1 teaspoon salt

¾ cup lard or vegetable shortening

1 large egg yolk, beaten

2 teaspoons apple cider vinegar

2 to 4 tablespoons ice water

In a food processor or bowl, combine flour and sugar. Add fat and pulse (or rub with fingers) until coarse crumbs form. Add egg, vinegar, and 2 tablespoons water and pulse (or mix with fork). Add additional tablespoons of water until dough holds together. When dough is moist enough to gather into a cohesive mass, divide dough into two flat, burger-shaped discs and wrap with plastic wrap. Refrigerate at least 30 minutes.

Roll dough out on a lightly floured surface to a ¼-inch thickness (or 13- or 14-inch round for a 10-inch pie plate) and place in pie plate. You should have a 1- inch overhang. Crimp edges decoratively for a single crust or fill and top with another crust as directed.

Makes one 9- or 10-inch double-crust pie

Extra-Tart Apple Crisp

Since West Virginia is such a big apple-growing state there were always a lot of desserts made with them. And a crisp is one of the easiest. Opal had an ancient, "early" apple tree in her yard that bore small, very tart chartreuse green apples. I occasionally see the apples—sometimes called "June" apples—at the local farmer's market in summer and I snap them up, turn them into applesauce, and freeze for later. They also make a great apple crisp topped with oats and nuts that is wonderfully crunchy and earthy. Serve the crisp warm with vanilla ice cream or plain whole-milk yogurt mixed with a little maple syrup (which is good for breakfast). Granny Smith apples are nearly as tart and work nicely too.

1 cup old-fashioned rolled oats

⅓ cup sliced almonds

⅓ cup all-purpose flour

⅓ cup packed light brown sugar

2 teaspoons ground cinnamon

5 tablespoons unsalted butter, cut into small cubes

2½ pounds tart apples such as Granny Smith, or greening, peeled, cored, and thinly sliced

¼ cup granulated sugar

¼ teaspoon freshly grated nutmeg

1 tablespoon lemon juice

Preheat oven to 375 °F.

In medium bowl combine the oats, almonds, flour, brown sugar, and 1 teaspoon of cinnamon. Scatter butter over oat mixture. Using your fingertips, blend butter into dry ingredients until the mixture forms large clumps.

In a 9- or 10-inch glass pie dish or 9-inch baking dish, combine the apples, granulated sugar, nutmeg, lemon juice, and remaining teaspoon of cinnamon. Sprinkle oat topping evenly over apples. Bake 40 to 45 minutes, or until apples are tender and the topping is golden brown.

Makes one 9- or 10-inch crisp
Serves 6 to 8

Half-moon Apple Pies

....

Fried pies are an Appalachian tradition, for they did not depend upon seasonal fruit (the filling is made from dried apples) and they were highly transportable, easily packed into a coal miner's lunch pail. Opal was famous for her pies and always dried her own apples, but the ones in the natural-food store work just fine. Using apple cider in lieu of water to reconstitute them gives them a more intense apple flavor. You can also make the pies using dried peaches, or a combination of dried fruits (such as apples and raisins), but I prefer it with plain apples. I've included instructions for baking and for frying the pies. Frying the pies makes the flakiest crust you've ever experienced and I strongly recommend trying it at least once for a treat.

8 ounces (about 4 cups, packed) dried apples	½ teaspoon nutmeg
	½ cup sugar
4 cups apple cider or apple juice	1 Flaky Piecrust (recipe page 80)
1 teaspoon ground cinnamon	confectioners' sugar for dusting

Place the dried apples in a medium saucepan and add cider just to cover. Bring to a simmer and cook (adding more liquid, if necessary), until just tender, about 20 to 30 minutes. Add the spices and sugar and stir until sugar dissolves. Remove from heat and cool completely. (Applesauce can be made several days in advance and refrigerated.)

Roll out chilled dough on a lightly floured surface to a ¼-inch thickness. Using a 4½-inch saucer as a template, cut out circles with a sharp knife.

Place about 2 tablespoons of the applesauce in the center of the dough circle. Moisten edges of dough with a little water. Fold dough over to make a half-moon shape. Press edges together with the tines of a fork. Repeat with remaining dough and applesauce. If you have time, refrigerate the pies 30 minutes to 1 hour before baking or frying. The crust will be less likely to crack.

To Bake Half-moon Pies:

Heat oven to 375°F. Place the pies on an ungreased baking sheet and brush lightly with water. Bake for 20 to 25 minutes, or until tops are golden brown. Transfer to wire racks to cool until warm to the touch. Sprinkle with confectioners' sugar just before serving.

Variation for Fried Half-moon Pies:

Add enough vegetable oil in an iron or electric skillet to measure ½-inch deep. Heat the oil until hot, but not smoking (about 375 °F, or when a small scrap of dough turns golden in 30 seconds). Working in small batches, slip the pies into the hot oil using a large spatula, gently pushing the pie off the spatula with a butter knife. Fry the pies until golden brown, about 5 minutes each side. Drain on layers of paper towels. Cool until warm to the touch. Sprinkle with confectioners' sugar just before serving.

here's what's cookin'

FRESH APPLE CAKE

recipe from: EDNA GANDEE

serves:

2 cups sugar
1 cup cooking oil
3 eggs
2-¼ cups flour
2 tsp. soda
½ tsp. salt

1 tsp. cinnamon
1 tsp. allspice
1 tsp. nutmeg
1 cup buttermilk
1 tsp. vanilla
1-½ cups grated apples
1 cup chopped nuts

oil & eggs together
ingredients together.
buttermilk and
mixture. Combine well.
walnuts. Pour into
inch tube pan.
350° oven.

¼ cup orange
sugar. mixed with 1 cup confectioner's
Pour over cake while
hot.

Peach-Raspberry Half-moon Pies

This is a version of the pies using fresh fruit and baking them. These are perfect to pack for a summer picnic when peaches are at their peak.

3 cups all-purpose flour

2 tablespoons sugar

¼ teaspoon salt

1 cup (2 sticks) cold unsalted butter, cut into small pieces

6 to 8 tablespoons ice water

1 cup soft white bread cubes (crusts trimmed)

1 tablespoon melted butter

1½ cups peach or apricot preserves

2 medium peaches, peeled and diced

½ cup fresh raspberries

Place the flour, salt, and sugar in the large bowl of a food processor fitted with a metal blade. Add the butter and pulse the mixture a few times until it resembles coarse cornmeal. Add 6 tablespoons of the ice water and pulse about 3 times just till the dough clings together.

Refrigerate the dough at least 30 minutes. Roll dough out on a lightly floured surface to a ¼-inch thickness. Using a 4½-inch saucer as a template, cut out circles with a sharp knife.

Toss the bread crumbs with the melted butter. Mix together with the preserves and peaches. Place 3 tablespoons of the mixture in the center of each dough circle. Top with 4 berries. Moisten edges of dough with water. Fold dough over to make a half-moon shape. Press the edges together with the tines of a fork. Repeat with the remaining dough and pie filling. Transfer pies to an ungreased baking sheet. Refrigerate 30 minutes.

Preheat oven to 375°F. Bake 20 to 25 minutes, or until edges and tops are golden brown. Transfer pies to wire racks to cool.

Makes 20 pies
Serves 20

Reva J.'s Peach Dumplings

This recipe comes from my mother's friend and fellow Cake Club member Reva Johnson. They're very easy to make and best with large, summer-ripe peaches from the farmstand.

2 cups all-purpose flour

2 teaspoons baking powder

½ teaspoon salt

1 stick cold unsalted butter

½ cup milk

8 large ripe peaches

Syrup:

1½ cups granulated sugar

2 cups water

1 tablespoon butter

1 3-inch stick cinnamon

Preheat oven to 375°F. Stir together the flour, baking powder, and salt. Using the large holes of a box grater, grate the butter over the flour. Use your fingers to break the butter into smaller bits, like coarse meal. Add the milk, a little at a time, and stir with a fork until a dough forms.

Roll the dough out on a lightly floured surface to ¼-inch thickness. Cut into strips about 8 inches long and 2 inches wide. Cover with plastic wrap and chill while you prepare peaches.

Peel the peaches and slice a little off the bottom so peaches will stand up. Place in a bowl of cold water with lemon juice in it to prevent them from turning brown.

Remove peaches and pat dry but don't pit (this adds flavor and keeps it intact). Cut two 2-inch squares of pastry for top and bottom of peach. Then join with a long strip, pressing seams together to enclose the peach. Refrigerate 30 minutes. Place dumplings on a lightly greased baking sheet. Lightly brush with water and sprinkle with sugar. Bake 25 to 35 minutes, until golden brown.

Meanwhile, place syrup ingredients in a medium saucepan and bring to a boil. Boil 10 minutes, remove from heat. Serve the dumplings hot with ice cream and the syrup drizzled over.

Serves 8

A Good Man Really Is Hard to Find (Especially in Nashville, Tennessee)

I once cooked dinner for a man with the hope that he would fall in love with me. Brilliant, right? Actually, I did this way more than once, but this time in particular was the most futile of all.

The lost cause in question was, predictably, a tall, dark Texan with dust on his boots and a shock of curly hair, seemingly too wild to tame (both him and the hair, that is). The perfect challenge. I imagined myself the ideal woman for him, of course, independent, none too demanding (God forbid), and a good cook to boot. I planned to ensnare him with Southern charm and a killer dessert.

The romance had started out awkwardly enough. He knew my boyfriend—that is, my dumped-as-soon-as-I-met-this-guy boyfriend. At the time I was a newspaper reporter and we'd had lunch on the pretense of my researching a story and, sure enough, wound up in bed. It was exciting. Meeting him in a dark studio late at night—where his band, including a sexy chanteuse who took deep swigs of Courvoisier between takes, a famous producer, and a *New York Times* critic made up the entourage—I believed was the *height* of coolness. And I was The Girlfriend, the "nicest, prettiest, and smartest girl" he had ever known. How could I resist?

This went on for two or three months, before he left to play a date in L.A. There were the passionate nightly phone calls at first which wound down, slowly, to nary a peep from the creep.

When he finally returned I invited him over for a proper dinner to celebrate the completion of his album. He brought along a cassette of the final version. It seemed cozy and familiar, so why was I such a wreck? Was I right in thinking my girlfriend shift was over (replaced perhaps by an even nicer, prettier, and smarter one?). Could it be he only wanted and needed me for the time it took to record a sixty-five-minute record? I was having doubts we'd make it through the tour. I'd spent the better part of that day obsessing over every single detail of the evening, down to the pressed sheets and the flowers in the bathroom. In spite of a case of heart palpitations and sudden onset of irritable bowel syndrome, I did manage to make him a rare steak (just as he liked it), and roast potatoes as crisp as a starched shirt.

For dessert I made both a lemon and a chocolate pie because you can never be sure if a man likes chocolate. It took even longer because I'd diced the butter and shortening into teeny tiny bits with a knife (no man's worth that but it does make an incredibly flaky crust). And it was, all of it, perfect.

He raved about the meal and liked both pies equally well. In my fantasies this is the part where he fell to one knee in a kind of food-induced love trance—just like a Sandra Bullock movie—to promise me his undying devotion and carry me back to his house in Texas. This house that he had so painstakingly restored, I had heard much about. So much that I could even see myself there in the kitchen with the gingerbread detailing, cooking on the old Garland stove as he strummed the guitar at the table. But of course none of that happened. My short-term objective—that he would stay the entire night (something he never did because of the late recording sessions)—was achieved. He left the next morning never to darken my door again. Like most cowboys (and musicians), he was more interested in moving on than moving in. And when he called one last time on a stopover on the tour, I finally said no. Oh, and the part about me being The Girlfriend was way off. As I later found out, there were others playing that role, all simultaneously (how *did* he manage?). Once I scraped myself off the floor, my best girl-friend Kay took me out for a drink, and told me everything.

"For God's sake, Susie, didn't you ever *listen* to his songs?" was all she said and needed to. In one, he pulls out a gun and shoots a former girlfriend on her wedding day. (Yeah, I kind of overlooked a couple of things when I was being swept away.)

A few years later he married a famous (and barefoot) actress and it made all the tabloids. And then my ultimate revenge fantasy came true when she dumped him. Yee-ha!

And now to my *Sex and the City* ending: I've since set aside notions of seduction by pie and now reserve my special efforts for someone who's willing to stick around long enough to dust his boots off. Or at least long enough to cook me breakfast.

All Kinds of Pies

Lemon Meringue Pie

My father's aunt Julia was at the top of our short list of relatives we'd jump in the car to go visit, which should tell you something about her cooking. This is her recipe for lemon meringue pie. It's fairly classic — firm and tart—and aims to please even if you're not trying to seduce someone.

1 prebaked 9-inch Butter Piecrust
(recipe follows)

Filling:

1 cup sugar	4 large egg yolks
5 tablespoons cornstarch	1 tablespoon unsalted butter
¼ teaspoon salt	½ cup freshly squeezed lemon juice
1 cup water	2 teaspoons finely grated lemon zest
½ cup milk	

Meringue:

4 large egg whites	pinch of salt
¼ teaspoon cream of tartar	½ cup sugar

Preheat oven to 350°F.

Make filling: In a heavy saucepan whisk together sugar, cornstarch, and salt. Gradually stir in water and milk, until the cornstarch dissolves. In a bowl whisk together yolks. Place the saucepan over medium heat, stirring, until it comes to a boil. Gradually whisk in 1 cup of the hot milk mixture into the beaten yolks. Pour the yolk mixture back into the saucepan and whisk until mixture boils again. Lower heat and simmer, stirring all the while, 3 minutes. Remove from heat and whisk in the butter, lemon juice, and zest until the butter melts. Cover the surface of the filling with buttered waxed paper to prevent a skin from forming.

Make meringue: In a bowl with an electric mixer, beat egg whites with cream of tartar and salt until soft peaks form. Slowly add the sugar in a stream, beating, until stiff peaks form.

Remove waxed paper and pour the warm lemon filling into the prebaked pie shell, smoothing the top. Spread the meringue over top, covering it completely and sealing it to piecrust edges. Make swirling peaks on top. Bake until the meringue is golden and crusty on top, about 15 minutes. Serve it warm, room temperature, or chilled.

Makes one 9-inch pie
Serves 6 to 8

There was a good deal of cake in the box; a great loaf of fruit cake, and two frosted loaves of pound cake, and half the round sponge cake that had been made for tea the evening before, beside some pieces that had been cut and not eaten. But Milly had been told she must not eat any cake unless some one [sic] gave it to her. She never must take it herself.

"I shall tell Grandma I didn't ask her because she was asleep," she thought; "she always gives it to me," and she took two pieces out and locked the little door again and crept softly upstairs.

—Sarah Orne Jewett, "Cake Crumbs"

Butter Piecrust

This is a sweet butter crust that turns a pretty golden color when baked. It is a good basic crust for most pies, particularly those requiring prebaked crusts. It also freezes well, but wrap it first in plastic wrap, then in foil, and date it. Try to use it within three months.

1½ cups all-purpose flour	½ cup (1 stick) unsalted butter,
1 tablespoon sugar	chilled, cut into small pieces
¼ teaspoon salt	4 to 5 tablespoons ice water

In a food processor or bowl, combine flour and sugar. Add butter and pulse (or rub with fingers) until fine crumbs form. Add 4 tablespoons water and pulse (or mix with fork) until dough holds together. (If necessary, add a little more water.) When dough is moist enough to gather into a cohesive mass, divide dough into two flat, burger-shaped disks and wrap with plastic wrap. Refrigerate at least 30 minutes.

Roll dough out on a lightly floured surface to a ¼-inch thickness (or 13-inch round for a 9-inch pie plate) and place in pie plate. You should have a ½-inch overhang. Crimp edges decoratively for a single crust or fill and top with another crust as directed.

To prebake crust: After crimping edges, prick shell in several places with a fork and chill, covered, for 30 minutes. Preheat oven to 400°F. Line shell with waxed paper and fill with rice, pie weights, or dried beans. Bake shell in middle of oven for 10 minutes. Carefully remove paper with rice, weights, or beans, and bake until golden, about 12 minutes more. Transfer to a rack to cool before filling.

To blind-bake crust: Follow directions for prebaking as above. After removing weights, bake only 5 minutes.

Makes one double crust for a 9- or 10-inch pie, or 2 single crusts

The Best Chocolate Cream Pie

(AND THAT'S NO LIE)

My friend Kathy Snyder is a member in good standing in my personal cake club. We share a love for desserts and saddlebred horses, which can be a deadly combo when you're trying to pull on your riding jods. This is her simple but fabulous recipe, which makes a very silky, rich chocolate pie.

1 prebaked 9-inch Butter Piecrust (recipe page 76)	4 large egg yolks
1 cup sugar	2 cups milk
4 tablespoons cornstarch	2 tablespoons unsalted butter
6 tablespoons unsweetened cocoa	1 teaspoon vanilla extract
pinch of salt	sweetened whipped cream
	chocolate shavings, optional

Prepare piecrust as directed and cool completely.

To prepare filling: Combine the sugar, cornstarch, and cocoa in a medium saucepan. Whisk together the yolks and milk in a bowl and gradually stir into the cocoa mixture. Place over medium heat and cook, stirring constantly, until mixture thickens and comes to a boil. Remove from heat and stir in the butter and vanilla. Spoon into cooled pie shell. Place buttered waxed paper directly on top of filling. Refrigerate at least 1 hour. Top with dollops of whipped cream and shaved chocolate before serving.

Makes one 9-inch pie
Serves 6 to 8

Coconut-Banana Cream Pie

I can't decide if I like banana or coconut cream pie best so I just combined the two for one super-deluxe pie.

1 prebaked 9-inch Butter Piecrust
(page 76)

Filling:

4 tablespoons cornstarch

pinch of salt

½ cup sugar

4 large egg yolks

2¾ cups whole milk

1½ teaspoons vanilla extract

2 tablespoons unsalted butter

¾ cup sweetened, flaked coconut

2 firm-ripe bananas

Topping:

1 cup heavy cream

2 tablespoons sugar

1 teaspoon vanilla extract

Prepare piecrust as directed and cool completely.

To prepare filling: In a medium saucepan, whisk together the cornstarch, salt, and sugar until there are no visible lumps. Beat the eggs yolks into the milk. Slowly whisk the egg-milk mixture in a stream into the cornstarch mixture over medium heat. Whisk all along the bottom and sides of the pan continuously until the mixture comes to a boil. Reduce heat to low and stir until the custard becomes thickened, about 3 to 5 minutes. (The filling will seem a bit thin, but it will become firm as it cools.)

Remove the pan from heat and stir in the butter and the vanilla. Place a circle of waxed paper over the top of the filling, pressing down so that no air is trapped; cool 30 minutes.

Remove waxed paper and fold in ½ cup of the coconut. Slice the bananas ¼-inch thick. Fold the bananas into the filling and pour it into the shell.

Use a hand mixer to whip the cream, sugar, and vanilla till it holds firm peaks. Spread the cream over the filling, making sure it touches the edges of the pastry all around. Toast the remaining ½ cup of coconut and cool, and sprinkle it over the top. You can refrigerate the pie several hours before serving time, but allow it to warm slightly before serving.

Makes one 9-inch pie
Serves 6 to 8

Flaky Piecrust for a Single Deep-Dish Pie

1½ cups all-purpose flour

1 tablespoon sugar

¼ teaspoon salt

6 tablespoons cold, unsalted butter, cut into small pieces

2 tablespoons cold vegetable shortening

1 large egg yolk, beaten

2 to 3 tablespoons ice water

Food processor method: Place all the ingredients except the yolk and water into a food processor and pulse at 1-second intervals until the mixture resembles coarse cornmeal. Add the egg yolk and sprinkle 2 tablespoons of water over the flour-butter mixture and pulse until the dough begins to clump together (add a little more water, if necessary).

Hand method: Stir together the flour, sugar, and salt in a large bowl. Add the butter and shortening, and, using your fingertips or a pastry blender, blend the fats into the flour until the mixture looks like coarse crumbs. Add the egg yolk and sprinkle water over the flour-butter mixture; stir with a fork to incorporate the water (it will still seem rather clumpy, but should hold together).

Turn the dough out onto a large piece of plastic wrap. Using your hands, gather the dough together to form a ball. Press it with your palms to form a 1-inch-thick disk. Wrap it up and refrigerate for at least 30 minutes.

On a lightly floured surface with a floured rolling pin, roll the dough into a 15-inch circle. Place in a 10-inch (preferably glass), deep-dish pie plate. Trim away all but 1 inch of the overhanging dough. Turn it under the rim and flute the edges. Chill the piecrust 30 minutes, until firm. Proceed with recipe as directed above.

Makes enough for one double-crust 9- or 10-inch pie, or two single crusts

Driving Miss Minnie

. . . .

Minnie Pearl never said hello, and she never said good-bye. You'd pick up the phone and there she'd be. There was no mistaking the voice.

"Did I tell you to pick me up at eleven-thirty?" Then, without pausing for my answer, "Better make it eleven." Click.

Minnie worked the phone like a Wall Street broker, sitting in her sunny home office on Curtiswood Lane in Nashville, which is next door to the governor's mansion. Even in her mid-seventies, Minnie maintained a hectic schedule and micromanaged her career.

"Where do I need to be? . . . What time? . . . Full costume or just the hat?" Click.

At twenty-five, I could barely keep up. In addition to appearing on the Grand Ole Opry, Minnie donated her time to her favorite causes, visited her museum on Music Row daily, played bridge at the Belle Meade Country Club, and donned her tennis skirt at least three times a week. She was my mentor and idol, and adopted me as her wayward child whom she counseled in matters of business and love.

I initially knew Minnie (her real name was Sarah Cannon) only from *Hee Haw* episodes I had watched growing up. But I came to know her intimately when we worked together on a weekly column she wrote for the afternoon newspaper in Nashville about the early days of country music. As Minnie's co-writer, I visited her at her spacious California-style stucco house with pool and gardens, and tape-recorded her stories for the articles. By eight o'clock each morning Minnie was well into the day and I sat across from the desk as she answered a steady flow of calls. It was a cozy room with warm wood paneling, tastefully decorated in shades of yellow and green. There were handmade gifts from fans, countless photos of Minnie and friends, and the awards that testified to her years in show business.

Her personal style was the antithesis of her stage character. And I think most people would be amazed that she was an intellectual. She had a great flair for fashion. In *Minnie Pearl: An Autobiography* there is a photograph of Minnie and her husband, Henry Cannon, as he helps his bride into a car after their wedding in 1947. Minnie is dressed in a leopardskin coat, wool suit, alligator pumps, and matching handbag. She looks sexy, even glamorous, a far cry from her simple country character in a gingham dress, size ten Mary Janes, and trademark straw hat. Her good taste was still evident when I met her. She preferred tailored slacks, a silk blouse, a well-cut blazer, and pearls. Her years at an exclusive finishing school where she studied "dramatics" were still evident in her speech and manners.

She was never meant to be Minnie Pearl, she would often point out. The daughter of a successful lumberman in Centerville, Tennessee, Minnie and her sisters dressed in pristine white dresses trimmed in lace and attended the best schools. Her intention to pursue a career as a comedic theater actress following graduation was derailed during the post-Depression era, when a chance appearance on a radio show on which she played a naive hillbilly girl propelled her to a regular spot on the Grand Ole Opry and stardom. It was rare that a solo performer, let alone a woman who didn't front a band, performed on the show. But following her short stand-up act, the switchboard "lit up" with callers clamoring for more.

Before arriving at the Opry, though, Minnie had her share of tribulations. Her life plan had changed measurably after the family lumber business was lost. Minnie took a job traveling to small towns in the South to produce and direct the local "talent" in plays. She traveled alone with trunks of wardrobe and props, sometimes forced to share the bed with a young daughter of a host family. Once she was awakened in the middle of the night when an inebriated father mistook her for his daughter. She was about to scream when the daughter placed her hand over Minnie's mouth to quiet her. The girl slipped out of bed and did not return until morning.

Later, as a single woman traveling with all-male hillbilly bands, she told me she had witnessed things that would have driven her mother to an early grave. She did not tell me these stories for use in the columns we wrote but as life lessons from a woman with experience, wisdom, and a few battle scars. Minnie never hesitated to chastise me for some of my romantic interests, particularly if someone happened to be a musician. "You mustn't take them seriously," she'd say, annoyed that she had to remind me of this yet again.

The newspaper column usually wrote itself, as Minnie was an inveterate storyteller. After it was written I'd take a copy to her for her approval, often between one of her speaking engage-

ments or an Opry performance. As Minnie's driving had been curtailed due to her failing vision, I became her part-time chauffeur of sorts, driving Miss Minnie hither and yon in her yellow Eldorado. (For a time I was well-known at the Opryland security gates.) The column received short shrift and mostly I listened while she held forth on some interesting person she'd just met or a new novel. Minnie was a voracious reader and often loaned or gave me books she thought I ought to read. She would quote from novelist Ayn Rand's *Fountainhead* and the poetry of Edna St. Vincent Millay, two of her favorite writers. Often we'd go out to lunch, usually at a music business hangout where she got lots of attention. If the well-wisher was an attractive man, all conversation stopped as she focused completely on him. Minnie adored men and had a way of making them feel as if they were the most fascinating specimen she had ever met. She was still a sexy, attractive woman and relished these occasional flirtations: "My, but you're such a smart man. And soooo handsome—mercy!" To Minnie, this *was* lunch.

I loved being in her house when everyone was around. Mary Cannon (not related) was Minnie and Henry's longtime housekeeper who had been with them since they'd married. They knew each other's habits and temperaments and played off each other to comic effect. Minnie would yell "May-ree!" which was a signal to her that she'd misplaced her purse. Mary would show up a few minutes later, shaking her head and dangling the pocketbook from her finger (just like it had happened every day for fifty years, and it had).

Both Mary and Minnie were incredible cooks. Minnie, in fact, wrote her eponymous cookbook in 1970 and it's full of great southern classics. I still use it all the time. It includes Mary's hot-water corn cakes (shockingly good) and a beef stew with corn and lima beans. I tried replicating the stew from the cookbook many times but it never tasted like Mary's. Then one day Mary shared the secret (not in the cookbook)—a healthy dose of Maker's Mark, which was also Minnie's cocktail of choice. It beats Julia Child's beef bourguignonne hands down. Minnie

All Kinds of Pies

loved sweets. Oftentimes for our morning meetings, we'd share hot Krispy Kremes and Pepsi, or a little leftover blackberry cobbler. She also made a great chess pie (which follows), with a subtle lemon flavor and slightly chewy texture.

Our friendship continued beyond the life of the column when I moved to New York City. She had her doubts about my leaving: "I *worry* about you there," she wrote to me in a note she sent with an autobiography of a Southern writer (Celestine Sibley) titled *Turned Funny*, which is the way Minnie described herself. The last time I saw her was shortly before her debilitating stroke. I was visiting from New York and went to meet and take her to the Opry. She was outside, dressed in a bright blue checked dress, her hat tucked under her arm, working the *New York Times* crossword puzzle on the hood of the Eldorado. I drove her to meet fans at her museum, which was now located at Opryland as Mr. Gaylord (the owner of Opryland) had recently purchased it as a way to help Minnie keep it afloat. Afterward we went to the Opry stage, just a few steps away, where Minnie received her usual applause.

Driving home that evening, Minnie said she hated to see me go back to Manhattan. "That's where I would have gone at your age. To *Broadway*," she said. "But I couldn't get the Nashville dust off my shoes."

That was the last time I saw Minnie, but it ended the same way as always. Minnie said what she needed to say. She did not say good-bye.

When I think about Aunt Ambrosy's blackberry cobbler smothered with thick cream—I could purely write a poem. My own specialty is cakes, which allus turned Lizzie Tinkum frog-eyed with jealousy. (She's my best friend.) One day at an annual picnic, I seen Lizzie standin' over my cake ponderin' on it. I sez, "Lizzie, how come you're starin' at my sponge cake?" And she sez, sweeter'n new molasses—"I didn't know whether to slice it up or wring it out." Ain't that spiteful? I got even. I turned her upside down cake right side up!

—Minnie Pearl, *Minnie Pearl Cooks*

Minnie Pearl's Chess Pie

1 blind-baked 9-inch Butter Piecrust
(recipe page 76)

4 large eggs

1¼ cups granulated sugar

2 tablespoons cornmeal

4 tablespoons unsalted butter, melted

¼ cup fresh lemon juice

1 tablespoon finely grated lemon zest

¼ cup buttermilk

½ teaspoon salt

confectioners' sugar for dusting

Prepare piecrust and blind-bake it as directed. Cool completely.

Preheat oven to 375°F. Place the eggs in a large bowl. Begin beating on low speed with an electric mixer. Gradually add remaining ingredients and beat well until combined. Pour into the blind-baked pie shell. Place oven rack on lower third of oven. Place pie on bottom rack and bake 15 minutes. Reduce the heat to 350°F and bake 20 to 25 minutes more, or until sides are beginning to pull away from crust (the center may still be a little jiggly).

Transfer to a rack to cool. Serve warm or room temperature. Sprinkle with confectioners' sugar before serving.

Makes one 9-inch pie
Serves 6 to 8

Butternut Squash Pie

Aunt Martha only made one kind of pie (squash) and one kind of cake (hickory nut). Why? Because that's what she had on her farm. She was thrifty and self-reliant, Aunt Martha was. This is very simple, wholesome tasting pie and will remind you of a holiday pie, although the squash has a much fresher taste than pumpkin from a can. Instead of peeling and boiling the squash, it's easier to roast it and scoop out the flesh.

1 9-inch Flaky Piecrust (page 80)

1 (2-pound) butternut squash

½ cup packed light brown sugar

1 tablespoon robust molasses

½ teaspoon salt

½ teaspoon freshly grated nutmeg

1 teaspoon ground ginger

2 large eggs, beaten

¼ cup heavy cream or whole milk

1 tablespoon unsalted butter, melted

sweetened whipped cream

Prepare piecrust as directed and line pie plate; crimp edges, and refrigerate.

Preheat oven to 400°F. Slice the squash in half lengthwise and remove the seeds. Lightly spray or brush a foil-lined baking sheet with cooking oil. Place squash cut side down on sheet. Bake 35 to 40 minutes until soft. Cool until warm enough to handle. Scoop out flesh and refrigerate to cool completely. You should have about 3 cups mashed squash.

Preheat oven to 425°F. Combine the squash and remaining ingredients (except whipped cream) in a food processor until smooth and creamy. Pour into prepared piecrust. Bake 45 minutes until a knife inserted between the crust and the center comes out clean. (Check pie after 20 minutes; if necessary, cover edge of crust with foil to prevent overbrowning.) Transfer to a rack to cool. Serve with sweetened whipped cream.

Makes one 9-inch pie
Serves 6 to 8

Frozen Peanut Butter Pie

My mother always made this for my brother Joey, who could eat the entire thing in one sitting. Despite his Herculean appetite, the pie is very rich to the average palate and just a sliver is sufficient for normal people. You can make your own graham cracker crust or you can buy the one at the supermarket if time is short. It's a good dessert to make ahead and place in the freezer (two days at most) if you're planning a dinner party. If you really want an over-the-top dessert, drizzle it with a little chocolate sauce.

1 10-inch Graham Cracker–Nut Crust (recipe follows)

1 (8-ounce) package cream cheese, softened

¾ cup confectioners' sugar

½ cup milk

1 cup creamy, natural-style peanut butter

1 teaspoon vanilla extract

1 cup heavy cream

sweetened whipped cream

Place cream cheese, sugar, milk, peanut butter, and vanilla in a large mixing bowl and beat with an electric mixer until creamy.

In another bowl, whip the cream until stiff peaks form. With a rubber spatula, fold in peanut butter mixture. Scrape mixture into pie shell and spread to edges, smoothing top. Freeze pie, uncovered, at least five hours. Cover with foil until ready to serve. Remove from freezer and let stand 15 minutes at room temperature before serving. Garnish with dollops of whipped cream, if desired, and graham cracker crumbs.

Makes one 10-inch pie
Serves 6 to 8

Emma as a young working girl.

Graham Cracker–Nut Crust

Like everything, homemade graham cracker crust is so much better than purchased.

1 cup graham cracker crumbs
(10 cracker rectangles)

½ cup finely chopped unsalted
roasted peanuts or walnuts

⅓ cup butter, softened to room
temperature

2 tablespoons sugar

Preheat oven to 350°F. Blend the crumbs, nuts, butter, and sugar in a bowl. Firmly press the mixture on the bottom and sides of a buttered, 9- or 10-inch glass pie dish. Bake 8 to 10 minutes until the crust is lightly toasted. Cool to room temperature before filling.

Makes one, 9- or 10-inch crust

Frozen Caramel (Dulce de Leche) Pie

This is a dream of a caramel pie and so easy to make. Cooking condensed milk is common in many Spanish desserts and creates caramelized "dulce de leche." It does take time but there's no stirring required. You can put the pie together and pop it in the freezer the morning before a dinner party. It has a creamy, frozen mousse-like texture with a buttery crunch of candied walnuts on top.

1 (10-inch) Graham Cracker–Nut Crust
(recipe, page 88)
1 (14-ounce) can sweetened,
condensed milk

⅓ cup chopped walnuts
1 tablespoon unsalted butter
1 tablespoon granulated sugar
2 cups heavy whipping cream

Preheat oven to 400°F. Pour the milk into an 8-inch pie plate (preferably metal). Cover with foil. Place the pie plate in a larger pan and pour in about 1-inch of boiling water. Bake 1 hour and 20 minutes, or until the milk is thick and has a deep caramel color. Leave it covered and set aside to cool to room temperature (or place in the fridge to speed up the process).

In a skillet over medium heat, melt the butter and sugar. Add the nuts and cook, stirring, until coated and lightly golden brown. Set aside to cool.

Using an electric mixer, whip the cream till it holds stiff peaks. Add a large dollop of the whipped cream to the caramelized milk to lighten it. Then fold (but don't beat), the caramelized milk into the whipped cream until blended. Spoon the filling in the crust. Place in the freezer at least 2 hours, until solid. Remove from the freezer and scatter the candied walnuts on top. Slice the frozen pie and place on plates. Let pie slices sit out at room temperature for 15 minutes before serving.

Makes one 10-inch pie

We lived dangerously, sans sunscreen, on a
family vacation at Daytona Beach, Florida.
From left: Emma, Susie, Jim, and Linda.

Teatime Sweets

Lisa's Currant Scones

Ginger Muffins with Chocolate Glaze

Upside-Down Pear Honey Cakes

Candied Orange-Apricot Bread

Drop Biscuits

Fried Apples

Buttermilk Biscuits

Pecan Sticky Biscuits

Abigail's Sinful Whole Wheat Raisin, Banana, and Walnut Bread

Strawberry-Rhubarb Crumble Cake

Blackberry Bread Pudding

Light Custard Sauce

A Proper Tea

My friend Lisa is awesome. You notice this immediately as she is six feet tall and gorgeous. However, I should note that she is a professional gorgeous person for she was a famous runway star; her winsome smile and giraffe-length legs graced the pages of magazines for years. Lisa posed for many famous photographers (Horst, in fact, took a now-famous photo of her from the waist down dressed in nothing but a tutu, lace-topped stockings, garter, and spike heels). A few years ago she stepped *behind* the camera, and it was Lisa who photographed the food in my cookbook *Quick Simple Food*.

When I first moved to New York we were roommates, sharing a house upstate along with her daughter, Roxanne Marie, lovingly known as Cookie. We had a time in the old farmhouse she had bought when she retired from modeling at the wise old age of thirty, cooking incredible feasts and filling the place up with an assortment of local Woodstock types as well as our more urban friends from the city. We planted a garden, or rather we planted some vegetables around the rocks in the yard. We were, for a summer, earth mothers who had foresworn makeup, nail polish, and designer shoes for saris, halter tops, and bare feet. We recycled everything from the cat-food cans to laundry soap bottles and we were kind to nature and the planet in general. The three of us (and the occasional guest) did a lot of nude sunbathing to get even closer to nature, much to the delight of the elderly gentleman next door who may have been daft but certainly wasn't blind.

Even the pair of pampered Himalayan cats, Lucca and Louis, returned to nature and you could hear them at night, stalking and attacking a defenseless deer in the backyard (they squeal, you know). Nearly every day we'd find evidence of their hunting escapades: one morning at breakfast we all looked up from our tea simultaneously to see a giant dead bunny propped up in a corner missing its head. *Ew!*

One of our rituals was afternoon tea, and Lisa taught me the importance of doing it "properly" after I returned from the store one day with a box of dreadful Lipton's tea bags. "It tastes like paper, string, and staples!" she exclaimed. Being the hick from the hills, I was eager to learn all there was to know about making a "cuppa tea." Here is Lisa's technique as told to me, just so you won't make the same mistake I did and serve someone tea in a bag. You may notice she has a habit of channeling Dame Edna. We love Dame Edna.

My Story About a Proper Cup of Tea

BY LISA RUTLEDGE

Don't you just hate it when you go to a restaurant and order tea and it's brought to you this way: a cup of tepid water with a teabag floating in it. Then there's the question of what to do with that soggy bag afterwards? It's from you Yanks I learned how to wrap the tea bag string around the teaspoon and sort of squinch and squeeze the remaining tea out of the tired old thing. How revolting!

I grew up in Australia where "morning tea" was always at 10:00 A.M. or so. There was also afternoon tea and sometimes tea was taken with evening meal, too. With our tea we would munch on "bikkies" (or biscuits—Australians are famous for abbreviating everything), and I remember one sort of bikkie was actually called Morning Tea. Sometimes in the afternoon I would be given the task of whipping up a tea cake from a packet. It had butter and cinnamon on the top. *Yum.*

I really know how to make a very decent cup of tea; I stand alone here in the U.S.A. I'm sorry, but it's true. Please take note as I now share with you the process:

Warm your teapot by pouring hot water into it while you wait for your tea water to boil in the kettle. When the pot is nice and warm, empty the water out and put in one teaspoon of tea per person and one for the pot. Lovely. Allow the tea to "sweat" for a few moments. (I just made this part up but I think it adds something. . . .)

Bring freshly filtered water to a rolling boil—don't boil the life out of it, for heaven's sake—then pour it into your teapot. Allow about one cup of water per person. Steep for three to five minutes, max.

While the tea is steeping, pour a bit of milk into your tea cup (if you take milk, that is). Never cream or half-and-half, Yankees! Yes, you do this before you pour in the tea.

When the tea is ready, turn the pot seven times to the left then seven times to the right. No, really—I'm not kidding. Then pour it through a little tea strainer. Add your sugar or whatnot. Stir and place your teaspoon in your saucer. Yes, that's right: always drink your tea from a cup and saucer. Bone china is best.

Serve with an assortment of bikkies or little sandwiches made with white bread, with the crusts cut off if you want to be posh.

Now, isn't that a refreshing and delightful little ritual?

It was her habit to take a very slight refreshment at the usual tea hour, and supplement it by a substantial lunch at bed-time, and so now she was not only at leisure herself, but demanded the attention of her guests. She had evidently prepared an opinion, and was determined to give it. Miss Eunice grew smaller and thinner than ever, and fairly shivered with shame behind the tea-tray. She looked steadily at the big sugar-bowl, as if she were thinking whether she might creep into it and pull something over her head. She never liked an argument, even if it were a good-natured one, and always had a vague sense of personal guilt and danger.

—Sarah Orne Jewett, *A Country Doctor*

Lisa's Currant Scones

···

This is a good basic recipe for a tender scone to which you could add all sorts of "whatnot," as Lisa says. Scones are best eaten warm and are traditionally served with strawberry jam and clotted or Devonshire cream—a high-butterfat cream sometimes sold in nicer markets. Lisa says crème fraîche or sweetened whipped cream is a decent substitute.

2 cups bleached all-purpose flour

3 tablespoons sugar, plus additional
  for sprinkling

3 teaspoons baking powder

1/2 teaspoon baking soda

1/4 teaspoon salt

6 tablespoons cold unsalted butter, cut
  into small pieces

1/4 cup currants

1 tablespoon finely grated orange zest

2/3 cup buttermilk, plus additional for
  brushing

1/2 cup clotted cream, crème fraîche, or
  whipped cream, optional

strawberry jam, optional

Preheat oven to 425°F.

Sift together the flour, sugar, baking powder, baking soda, and salt. Add the butter and use a pastry blender or your fingers to work butter into the flour mixture until it resembles a coarse meal. Add currants and zest and toss in flour mixture to coat. Add the buttermilk and stir with a fork until dough holds together. Turn the dough out onto a floured board and knead dough gently about 1 minute. Pat out to an 8-inch round (about 1 inch thick). With a long sharp knife, cut into 4 even wedges. Then cut those in half to make 8 wedges.

Place the wedges on an ungreased baking sheet (or one lined with parchment paper) about 1 inch apart. Brush tops lightly with a little buttermilk and sprinkle with sugar. Bake 10 to 12 minutes, or until lightly browned on top. Cool on pan 5 minutes before serving (or transfer to a rack and cool completely). Serve with clotted cream and jam, if desired.

Makes 8 wedge-shaped scones

Ginger Muffins with Chocolate Glaze

This is a simple way to get a quick gingerbread fix. Just stir everything together and spoon into the muffin cups. The pepper may seem odd but it makes the muffins nicely spicy. You don't have to make the chocolate glaze but it really elevates them to something special.

6 tablespoons unsalted butter, melted

2 large eggs, beaten

1/2 cup robust molasses

3/4 cup packed light brown sugar

1 tablespoon ground ginger

1/8 teaspoon ground white pepper

1 1/4 cups all-purpose flour

1 teaspoon baking soda

1/4 teaspoon salt

2/3 cup buttermilk

Chocolate glaze:

1/3 cup semisweet chocolate morsels

2 tablespoons heavy cream

Preheat oven to 350°F. Grease a 12-cup muffin tin with butter (or line with paper cups).

Combine butter, eggs, molasses, and sugar in a large bowl and beat with a whisk until blended. Stir together the ginger, pepper, flour, baking soda and salt. Fold into the molasses mixture along with the buttermilk and stir until mixture is just incorporated. Divide between muffin cups. Bake 12 to 15 minutes until muffins pull away from sides and are firm to the touch. Cool in tin 5 minutes, then turn out onto a rack to cool.

Place the chips and cream in a small glass measuring cup. Place in microwave and heat on high 20 to 30 seconds until partially melted. Stir until smooth. Drizzle over the muffins before serving.

Makes 12 muffins

Upside-Down Pear Honey Cakes

2 tablespoons unsalted butter

4 tablespoons plus ½ cup sugar

2 firm-ripe Bartlett pears, cored and
  sliced thin

1½ cups cake flour (not self-rising)

1 teaspoon baking powder

¼ teaspoon salt

1 teaspoon ground cinnamon

½ teaspoon ground allspice

½ cup (1 stick) unsalted butter,
  softened

1 large egg

½ cup granulated sugar

3 tablespoons honey

1 teaspoon vanilla extract

⅓ cup milk

Combine butter and 4 tablespoons of the sugar in a large nonstick skillet over medium heat. Stir until sugar bubbles and begins to caramelize. Add pear slices a few at a time, cooking about 1 minute each side, just until they begin to soften. Transfer to a plate and set aside.

Preheat oven to 325°F. Butter a 12-cup muffin tin. Sift together flour, baking powder, salt, cinnamon, and allspice. Beat ½ cup butter and remaining ½ cup sugar until light and fluffy. Beat in egg and honey until blended. Mix together vanilla and milk. With the mixer on low speed, add flour mixture alternately with the milk just until dry ingredients are moistened (do not overmix).

Arrange 3 to 4 overlapping slices of pear on bottom of each muffin cup. (Reserve juices left from cooked pears.) Spoon about ¼ cup batter into each cup so that cups are about three-quarters full (you may have a little batter left over, but do not overfill cups). Bake 20 minutes, or until cakes have pulled away from sides and are golden brown around edges. Transfer to a rack and cool 10 minutes. Run a knife around edges of cakes to loosen them. Place a large baking sheet over the muffin tin and quickly invert the tin to release the cakes. Drizzle reserved pear juices over cakes. Transfer cakes to a serving platter. Serve warm or room temperature.

Makes 12 tea cakes

Candied Orange-Apricot Bread

This bright, citrus-flavored tea bread tastes even better if made the day before serving.

3 medium oranges, preferably organic

1 cup sugar

1½ cups chopped dried apricots

3 tablespoons minced crystallized ginger

2½ cups all-purpose flour

2 teaspoons baking powder

¼ teaspoon salt

½ cup (1 stick) unsalted butter, softened

2 large eggs

½ cup milk

1 tablespoon orange liqueur such as Cointreau or Grand Marnier

confectioners' sugar for dusting

Scrub the oranges with water and a drop of dish soap to remove any coating. Using a vegetable peeler, remove the outer, bright orange zest from the oranges. Thinly slice the zest into fine slivers. Combine zest and ½ cup water in a small saucepan and bring to a boil. Lower heat, cover, and simmer 5 minutes. Stir in ¾ cup of the sugar to dissolve. Add apricots and ginger; simmer 5 minutes longer (the fruit will be candied and sticky, with almost no liquid left). Remove from heat and cool to room temperature.

Preheat oven to 325°F. Butter a 9 × 5 × 3-inch loaf pan. Sift together flour, baking powder, and salt. Combine liqueur with milk; set aside. Beat the butter and remaining ¼ cup sugar with an electric mixer until light and fluffy. Add eggs one at a time, beating well. Beat in cooled orange-apricot mixture. Add flour mixture alternately with milk, beginning and ending with dry ingredients. Scrape batter into pan.

Bake 1 hour and 15 minutes, or until a wooden skewer or knife inserted comes out clean. Cool on a rack 10 minutes. Remove from pan and return to rack to cool completely. Wrap tightly with plastic wrap until ready to serve. Dust with confectioners' sugar before slicing.

Makes one 9 × 5 × 2 inch loaf
Serves 12 to 16

Aunt Martha's Kitchen

Aunt Martha thought it amusing that I'd come all the way from New York City to spend the night with her in her farmhouse. Aunt Martha was actually my great-aunt, sister to my father's mother, who died when he was six. In all the important ways she was my grandmother for she helped raise my father, and she was the person I longed to be with when I was feeling at odds with the world.

Earlier that morning from the upstairs bedroom I heard the antique gas oven door's telltale squeak as she slid a pan of biscuits inside. I continued to lie in bed beneath ten pounds of quilts listening to the hall clock's pendulum click back and forth. The scent of the biscuits and sassafras tea soon creeped up the stairs and curled inside my nostrils. The essence blended with the other comforting scents of the old house: the branches of sweet Annie drying on the iron bed in the next room and the fresh smell of the sheets on the bed, which Aunt Martha had washed in rainwater and ironed just for my visit. I love going into the doll-size closet in the guestroom and running my hands over the crisp white linens and pillowcases she'd stacked and tied together with ribbons. She always prided herself on her laundering. "I've had many a fine wash from the rain barrel," she says. Large drums caught the runoff from the gutters and she filled the tub of her washer with it, and watered her gardens with the rest.

Aunt Martha lived alone in her three-story house, surrounded by all the simple, beautiful things she had created. In the corner of my room was an overstuffed ice blue chair that she had upholstered. Downstairs on the daybed where she slept, she'd sewn together a patchwork of vintage fabrics that would have sold for a pretty penny in a Ralph Lauren store. My favorite item in the house was a large "tree" she made from an ancient cherry tree's root she dragged off

On the porch with Aunt Martha Burford.

the hill decades ago when WPA workers cut a swath across the property for the power lines. It was mounted so that the tendrils reached skyward. Aunt Martha had adorned it with found objects: seashells tied with twine, feathers from blue jays and pheasants, dried Chinese lantern pods, and little felt birds.

Evidence of her nurturing was everywhere—from a sweet potato vine that wound its way across a kitchen wall to encircle a window, to the glass terrariums filled with moss and tiny plants in the dining room. Except for a new side-by-side refrigerator in the kitchen, the house lacked signs of modernity, and looked much the same as it did when she and her husband, Uncle Lee, first built it in the early 1930s.

Even at 108 years of age, Aunt Martha still tended a good-size vegetable garden brimming with greens, string beans, tomatoes, and peppers. Surrounding it were cinder blocks filled with sprouting garlic, which kept away bugs and also kept Aunt Martha stocked in her favorite home remedy (she made it a habit to eat several raw cloves daily, chopped and mixed in peanut butter and spread on toast). Whenever we drove up to the house I would look for her in the gardens, dressed in her long apron and skirt with an old-fashioned sunbonnet tied beneath her chin, the flowered print long faded by the sun. And she was usually there, using her hoe as both a gardening tool and a cane as she cultivated the rows.

At one time she and Uncle Lee kept cattle and mules in the pastures, a large chicken coop, and whole fields of corn and vegetables. She maintained huge beds of perennials, all old-fashioned varieties of roses, irises, and lilies. Lush ferns surrounded the foundation. Most of the beds had naturalized now that she was older. Still, it was amazing what she was capable of at her age.

I heard the oven door open once more to retrieve the biscuits, and I shoved off the mountain of quilts and pulled on my jeans to hurry downstairs to her warm kitchen. I'd lived on raisin bagels for the two years I'd been in New York and the thought of having a real biscuit made my mouth water.

"What's for breakfast?" I asked, entering the kitchen. "Well," she drawled slowly, "just a little bacon and what have you." This morning "what have you" includes fried apples, peach preserves, and white gravy made from the bacon drippings. All of which are meant to be eaten with Aunt Martha's famous drop biscuits. Oh, how we loved them.

Later that evening I sat with Aunt Martha on the porch as the sun began to drop. She was in one of the large Adirondack chairs that she covered with cushions and armrests in a bright crazy-quilt pattern. She was so still that a titmouse landed on the chair arm where her hand rested.

Aunt Martha was quiet and thoughtful, deeply religious but never judgmental. Sometimes she read romance novels, though she preferred the lovers do no more than kiss in the end. She stopped watching television during Clinton's first term, disillusioned that someone she admired would be unfaithful. Once, when I had broken an engagement (pretty close to the wedding date), she defended me to my mother. We three were sitting on the porch and Emma was literally wringing her hands in exasperation. Aunt Martha, who never appeared agitated and had little patience for those who did, waited for my mother to finish. She looked at her, and said, "Emma, Susie is just *Susie*. You shouldn't let it upset you so." I think it was her way of telling my mother to accept who I was because there wasn't much chance of changing the person or the circumstances at that point. (And she had never warmed up to my fiancé.)

The day of my visit (perhaps sensing I was in need of a friend) she tell me a story about herself, which was rare. When she was sixteen a neighbor came courting her. Her father did not approve of the family, and let his daughter know about it. Still, the boy persisted, though from a distance. One day she noticed him astride his horse in a field across the stream that separated the farms. Aunt Martha went to the barn and tied a rope around the draft horse's halter and climbed on his back. She rode him to the stream's edge across from her beau. And then she urged the horse forward and splashed across the shallow stream. Aunt Martha was nearly blushing and she smiled broadly as she told this. When she returned home her father saw her wet skirts and knew where she had been. She never saw the boy again, she said, but often wondered what her life would have been like if she had run away with him.

I went back to New York a few days later. It wasn't long before my mother called to tell me that Aunt Martha had fallen and broken a hip chasing a Copperhead snake off the porch with a broom. She had to go and live with her surviving daughter (the other two had died of natural causes). She considered it a temporary situation and always longed to be back on the farm. I think it was the only time she ever seemed unhappy. She died two years later at the age of 110 and the paper ran a lengthy obituary. In it, her daughter Norma told of her mother's philosophy of life: *Work hard so you sleep well. Use moderation in all things. Trust in the Lord.*

Drop Biscuits

You can make these biscuits with a baby balanced on your hip. They get their name because all you do is drop the sticky batter into a hot skillet. Drop biscuits cry out for homemade jam or apple butter. Made with bacon drippings, their smoky flavor is good served with a hearty soup or stew. For tea biscuits, use melted butter instead of the drippings, and add a few teaspoons of sugar. Made this way they are excellent for a quick strawberry shortcake. In the fall, I love serving them with hot fried apples, which is a good side dish with roast chicken or ham, too.

2 cups all-purpose flour	4 tablespoons bacon drippings or
½ teaspoon salt	melted butter
2 teaspoons baking powder	¾ to 1 cup milk or buttermilk

Preheat oven to 425°F. Lightly grease an 8- to 9-inch heavy ovenproof skillet (preferably cast iron), and place in the oven to heat while making the batter.

In a large bowl, combine the flour, salt, baking powder, and bacon drippings (or butter) and stir with a fork. Add the buttermilk, stirring just until dry ingredients are moistened.

Remove the skillet from the oven. Drop by heaping tablespoonfuls into the skillet, so that biscuits just touch. Bake 10 to 12 minutes, or until biscuits are golden brown on top. Serve hot with butter, jam, or fried apples (recipe follows).

Makes about 10 to 12 cakey biscuits

Fried Apples

In our family, fried apples were often served for breakfast or alongside pork or chicken dishes. They're actually stewed rather than fried, and best cooked in a skillet or heavy pot. Use a firm apple that will hold its shape so you don't wind up with applesauce. Some people like to add a little cornstarch to thicken the apples, but to me the results are more like a pie filling. Fried apples are usually flavored with butter, and you can sweeten them to your liking. I often cook them with sugar and butter and if I want a little more sweetness, I add some honey at the end.

2 pounds apples such as golden delicious, Granny Smith, or gala, peeled, cored, and sliced

⅓ cup sugar

2 tablespoons unsalted butter

pinch of salt

3 tablespoons water, apple cider, or juice

honey to taste, optional

Place everything but the honey in a large iron skillet or heavy-bottomed saucepan. Cover and bring to a simmer over medium heat. Cook 10 to 15 minutes until apples are tender (there should be a lot of juice accumulated). Remove the lid and cook, uncovered, until the juices cook down and the apples are very tender. Don't stir the apples or they will turn mushy. Add honey, if desired, and serve hot or room temperature.

Serves 4 to 6

Buttermilk Biscuits

This is a good basic biscuit recipe. It has a very fine texture and a classic crusty golden top.

2 cups all-purpose flour

½ teaspoon salt

1 tablespoon baking powder

½ teaspoon baking soda

⅓ cup cold butter or lard

⅔ cup buttermilk

Preheat oven to 425°F.

In a large bowl, stir together flour, salt, and baking powder. Add the butter and, using a pastry cutter or fingertips, work the fat into flour until it resembles a coarse oatmeal.

Add the milk and stir with a fork until the dough holds together. Turn out onto a lightly floured surface and gently knead dough about 1 minute, or until dough is no longer sticky. Roll or pat dough to a 1-inch thickness. Using a biscuit cutter, cut into 2-inch rounds. Place on an ungreased baking sheet (or one line with parchment paper or foil) about 1 inch apart for crustier biscuits, closer together for soft-sided ones. Bake 10 to 12 minutes, or until lightly brown on top.

Makes about 16 biscuits

Pecan Sticky Biscuits

Here's another biscuit recipe, which was Emma's clever method for making a quick and easy yeast-free cinnamon roll. These little pinwheels are best when baked in cake pans so they remain soft on the sides. You can prepare them and put them in the pans the night before and then pop them in the oven the next morning. They're good for brunch or tea. The bottoms get nice and sticky.

1 batch Buttermilk Biscuit dough
   (recipe page 106)
2 tablespoons unsalted butter, melted

⅔ cup packed brown sugar
1 teaspoon cinnamon
¾ cup chopped pecans

Preheat oven to 425°F. Lightly grease two 8-inch round cake pans.

Prepare the biscuit dough as directed. After kneading, roll or pat the dough into a rectangle, about ¼-inch thick. Brush with melted butter. In a bowl toss together the sugar, cinnamon, and pecans. Spread mixture evenly over the dough. Lightly press mixture into dough with your hands. At one of the long edges, begin rolling the dough into a tight cylinder, jelly-roll fashion. Wrap in waxed paper or plastic wrap and place in freezer for 10 minutes.

Remove wrapping and with a sharp knife cut into 1-inch thick slices. Place cut side down in cake pans, about ½-inch apart. Bake 15 minutes, or until lightly browned on top. Serve warm.

Makes 12 to 14 biscuits

Wiccan Ways

My friend Abigail lived the heathen lifestyle I always longed for in college. Her colorful tales of communal living with the rigid vegans and practitioners of white witchcraft were an excellent diversion from our day jobs at a magazine. Here's her story and a favorite tea bread recipe, which would not have been politically correct in the Syn household:

In college I lived in sin. Now, I know what you're thinking. Big deal. Most nineteen-year-olds cross the line into questionable territory at some point. But I really lived in "Syn," or Synergy as it was commonly known on the Stanford campus.

The forty-some-odd person coed house (give or take a few "stuffers," nonpaying residents who we'd "stuff" on mattresses on the roof) was devoted to all causes left of center. Far left. Although not a prerequisite to residency, almost everyone was a vegetarian, and many were hardcore vegans. Honey was not even allowed in the homemade granola. We held tight to hippie traditions: we composted—and took pride in the fact that when the wind came from the south, the odor would waft into the backyard of our neighbor, a frat house. We conducted all house business by consensus, which meant that meetings to determine who slept where—in single, double, triple, or commune rooms—could last up to eight hours. We took turns cleaning the toilets (and peed in co-ed bathrooms long before Ally McBeal made it chic). And you could always count on a synner to make her voice heard at the liberal cause of the week. We grew our own veggies, and hot bread came out of the oven at midnight, just in time for a study break.

Some of our most talked-about rituals took place in the kitchen. Like other coopera-
tively run houses on campus, we took turns cooking for the entire house every night, in
kitchen crews of three or four. Mollie Katzen was our god. The head chef would submit
a menu to the produce chief and to the bulk food manager the week
before to order all the ingredients. Around 3:00 P.M. the cooking com-
menced. Ambitious synners tried their hand at rolling veggie sushi
while more sensible folk made staples like the seitan burrito bar.
Yum. What made Synergy stand out from the other co-ops was the
fact that our all-natural cooking inspired many synners to strip.
Long before the Naked Chef, we were cutting up tofu in
the buff. Outsiders often asked if we had special hair
nets, you know, for down there, wink, wink. Or if anyone
ever had to be treated for burns below? Much to their disappoint-
ment, nothing so scorching ever happened. At least not when I lived
in Syn.

Abigail's Sinful Whole Wheat Raisin, Banana, and Walnut Bread

This is an earthy, lightly sweet banana bread that freezes nicely. It makes a firm, rounded loaf that you can slice thinly and spread with cream cheese and top with fig jam to make lovely tea sandwiches.

1 cup dark raisins	1 cup mashed very ripe bananas
½ cup chopped walnuts, toasted	(about 2 bananas)
1 cup all-purpose flour	3 tablespoons milk
¾ cup whole wheat flour	6 tablespoons unsalted butter,
2 teaspoons baking powder	softened
½ teaspoon baking soda	⅓ cup packed light brown sugar
½ teaspoon salt	2 large eggs
1½ teaspoons ground cinnamon	1 teaspoon vanilla extract

Preheat oven to 375°F. Butter and flour an 8 × 4 × 2-inch loaf pan.

Place the raisins and walnuts in a small bowl and toss with 1 tablespoon of the flour. Stir together the remaining flour, whole wheat flour, baking powder, soda, salt, and cinnamon. Mix together the mashed bananas and milk in another bowl and set aside.

Beat the butter and sugar in a large bowl with an electric mixer until light and fluffy. Beat in the eggs, one at a time, beating well after each addition; stir in the vanilla. Fold in the flour and banana-milk mixtures by hand using a large spatula until just blended. Then fold in the raisins and walnuts (do not overmix). Spoon the batter into the prepared pan. Bake the loaf 45 to 55 minutes, or until a wooden skewer inserted in the center of the loaf comes out clean. Cool on a rack 10 minutes. Run a butter knife around the edges then remove from the pan and place on a rack to finish cooling.

Makes one 8 × 4 × 2-inch loaf, or 12 muffins
Serves 10 to 12

Strawberry-Rhubarb Crumble Cake

....

The recipe for this fabulous coffee or snack cake has three parts, but it's well worth the effort. You can make the filling and crumb topping ahead of time, and then stir together the cake and assemble the morning you wish to serve it. Just the thing for a Sunday brunch. Thawed frozen strawberries work well if you want to save time.

Filling:

1½ cups diced rhubarb

2 cups (1 quart) hulled strawberries, crushed

1 tablespoon fresh lemon juice

½ cup granulated sugar

3 tablespoons cornstarch

Topping:

½ cup slivered almonds

6 tablespoons unsalted butter, cold

¾ cup all-purpose flour

½ cup packed light brown sugar

Cake:

½ cup (1 stick) unsalted butter, softened

¾ cup granulated sugar

2 large eggs

1 teaspoon almond extract

½ cup buttermilk

1½ cups all-purpose flour

1 teaspoon baking powder

½ teaspoon baking soda

confectioners' sugar for dusting

To make the filling: Combine the rhubarb, strawberries, and lemon juice in a medium saucepan over medium heat. Cover and cook, stirring occasionally, 5 minutes. Stir together the sugar and cornstarch and add to pan. Bring to a boil, stirring constantly, until rhubarb is tender and thickened. Remove from heat and cool to room temperature in refrigerator.

To make the topping: Combine topping ingredients in the bowl of a food processor and pulse a few times to combine (mixture should be crumbly). Refrigerate while you make cake.

To make the cake: Preheat oven to 375°F. Butter a 9-inch square baking pan. Cream the butter, sugar, egg, and extract in a large bowl with an electric mixer until light and creamy. Beat in the buttermilk. Stir together the flour, baking powder, and baking soda. With mixer on low, slowly add the butter mixture until just blended. Scrape batter into prepared pan.

Spread cooled filling on top of batter. Scatter the crumb topping over the filling. Bake 45 to 50 minutes, until the cake seems firm in the center and the edges are brown and pull away from the sides of the pan. Cool in pan on a rack until barely warm, or room temperature. Lightly dust with confectioners' sugar and cut into 6 to 9 squares before serving.

Makes one 9-inch square cake
Serves 6 to 9

"I cooked some rhubarb last week, and I told this woman up on Sylvan Lake, 'You could have heard me smacking my lips if you had been out on the porch. . .' That was the best stuff I ever put in my mouth! Oh, that was good!"

—Ione Dickerson, as quoted in The Foxfire Book of Appalachian Cookery

Blackberry Bread Pudding

For this recipe use day-old bread and choose large, plump berries, which are less seedy. Make the sauce first—even the day before is fine—and reheat it before serving.

Light Custard Sauce (recipe follows)

4 cups 1-inch cubes of day-old country white bread

4 tablespoons butter, melted

2 cups whole milk

¾ cup heavy cream

⅓ cup granulated sugar

2 teaspoons pure vanilla extract

¼ teaspoon freshly grated nutmeg

3 large eggs

3 tablespoons light brown sugar

1 pint plump blackberries

Toss the bread cubes with half of the melted butter. In a large bowl, whisk together the milk, cream, granulated sugar, vanilla, nutmeg, and eggs until well blended. Add the bread cubes to the bowl and let stand 15 minutes.

Preheat oven to 325°F and butter a 9-inch square baking dish or a shallow 2-quart casserole. Heat the remaining butter and brown sugar in a large nonstick skillet over medium heat until the mixture begins to simmer and the sugar dissolves. Remove from heat and add the berries and stir to coat. Gently stir into the soaked bread cubes. Transfer to the baking dish. Bake 45 minutes, or until a knife inserted in the center comes out clean. Cool in the pan on a wire rack about 30 minutes. Cut into 6 or 8 even slices. Spoon a pool of sauce onto each dessert plate and place a slice of the pudding on top. Pour a little more sauce over the pudding.

Serves 6 to 9

Light Custard Sauce

This custard sauce is lighter than most; the bread pudding is rich enough on its own without adding a heavy sauce. It is also delicious poured over warm apple pie or crisp.

2½ cups low fat milk

1 vanilla bean, split, or 2 teaspoons vanilla extract

1 strip orange zest

2 large eggs

⅓ cup sugar

Rinse a nonreactive saucepan with cold water and shake dry (this helps prevent sticking). Add the milk, vanilla bean, and orange zest, and bring the mixture almost to a boil. Remove from heat, cover, and set aside to steep for 30 minutes.

Return the milk to a simmer. Meanwhile whisk the eggs and sugar in a bowl until smooth but not fluffy. Gradually whisk in about half of the hot milk to warm the eggs, then pour all of the egg mixture into the simmering milk. Cook the custard over low heat, stirring constantly, until the mixture thickens enough to coat the back of a spoon, about 7 to 8 minutes (do not let the sauce boil).

Strain the custard into a clean bowl. Scrape the seeds from the vanilla bean into the custard or stir in the vanilla extract, if using. Cool in the refrigerator. Once chilled, cover the bowl with plastic wrap until ready to use (sauce will keep about 3 days).

Makes about 2³/4 cups sauce

Cookies and Candies

Russian Tea Crescents

Coconut–Chocolate Chip Macaroons

Becca's Almond Macaroons

Chocolate Chip Meringues

Butter Pecan Cookies

Chocolate-Covered Cherryettes

Emma's Molasses Crinkles

Sister's Big Buttermilk Sugar Cookies

Lemon Cookie Icing

Germaine's Mint Brownies

Butterscotch-Banana Blondies

Blu Baugh Bakery Hermits

Peanut Butter Shortbread

Crispy Treats

Chocolate Turtles

Cookies and Candies

Like most people, I don't think much about stirring up a batch of cookies or candy until the holidays. Then I go nuts. I'm usually visiting at my mom's, and I wait until I get there to start baking, as I like to get Emma's free expert advice. It can get a bit tense at times with the two of us in *her* kitchen, usually on matters of sugar as Emma uses her time-tested recipes and I am always experimenting, sometimes with good results, sometimes not. I will never be the baker my mother is but I enjoy making up cookie boxes to give to my friends and cousins.

It was the holiday baking that I enjoyed watching most when I was growing up. Emma has giant tins that start to fill the week before D-Day (Christmas) with a vast assortment of cookies, all pretty much perfect, the result of forty years' experience.

However, baking is just one of the things my mother does well, an example of her industrious soul. I worry that I've given you an incomplete picture of my mother, for she is more than a perfectionist who thinks Martha Stewart's cake decorating skills could use some polish. Emma excelled in school and had a scholarship to the local college but had to forgo further schooling in order to get a job and help support her parents. For a time she worked as a secretary, then in rapid succession, met and married a handsome war hero and had my brother, Joey. The marriage, though, was not a good one as her husband liked playing cards a lot more than going to work and bringing home a paycheck. After Emma came home one too many times to an empty house (he'd sold all the furniture and her wedding rings to pay gambling debts), she took action. She talked her husband into reenlisting in the army and when he was settled in Texas, she filed for divorce. As expected, once he was having fun with his army buddies, he didn't put up much of a fuss about the divorce. (I love how shrewdly she played him like a fiddle.)

My mother is tall, large boned, and sturdy as a rock. With coal black hair, hazel eyes, and a chiseled nose and cheekbones, she was quite striking, though shy about her beauty. She worked on the farm side by side with her mother and father, and helped raise her younger siblings. The family did not have much; for years Emma studied by the light of an oil lamp as there was no electricity until she was in high school. She was quiet and worked diligently and earnestly at all her chores.

Emma always approached cooking like a steelworker in a forge. She moved quickly with deft hands, sometimes singing an old song (she has a good voice). The motor of her Kitchen Aid mixer seemed to be always running, and there was something either going in or coming out of the oven most any time of day. My mother has never owned a mop, and scrubbed the floors by hand with a vengeance. If she cut her finger while chopping, she simply wrapped it in a paper towel and continued, waiting until dinner was on the stove before she got a bandage. Gardening, her other passion, was approached with this same kind of fervor and she spent hours at our childhood home designing and arranging her rock garden. We had dozens of varieties of iris and succulents, which were her favorites. Whenever we went on a road trip the car would be weighted down with river rocks to add to the landscaping. It was like a treasure hunt and we loved discovering an unusual one that would make her happy.

Before I was born, she worked very hard as a single mother to support herself and her parents as well. She met my father, who also had a son from a prior marriage, a few years after her divorce and they married. After my sister and I came along, she no longer worked outside the home.

You could see my mother through the kitchen window as you walked home from school or returned at dusk from playing with friends. Sometimes she would be rolling out leftover piecrust and sprinkling it with cinnamon-sugar for our after-school snack. We knew she would be there waiting for us in the kitchen, listening to her radio with a fresh pitcher of iced tea, always ready to hear about how our day went at school. While we told her about the latest drama, she would continue cooking . . . always cooking.

All of this is to say that you can imagine what a woman with this kind of energy could do with a little batch of cookie dough. This chapter includes a roll call of my mother's holiday favorites, including a few candies, and a few of my own.

Russian Tea Crescents

These are everyone's favorite cookie at Christmas. Tender and barely sweet, they are an elegant cookie that is very good with tea. The recipe calls for almonds but pecans or walnuts can be used instead.

1 cup (2 sticks) unsalted butter, softened

2¼ cups all-purpose flour

1 teaspoon vanilla extract

½ cup confectioners' sugar, plus additional for dusting

½ teaspoon salt

¾ cup very finely chopped natural almonds

Place all ingredients in a large bowl and stir together to incorporate (add a little water if it seems too dry). Cover with plastic wrap and refrigerate at least 1 hour.

Preheat oven to 350°F. Line a baking sheet with parchment or foil. Place a large piece of wax paper on the counter. Spoon tablespoons of dough onto the waxed paper. Roll each into a cigar shape, tapered at the ends (about 3 inches long). Fold cigars into a crescent shape and place on the baking sheets, about 1 inch apart. Bake 18 to 20 minutes until cookies are firm and just a little golden on the ends. Remove from oven and let cool 1 to 2 minutes, until firm enough to move.

Transfer hot cookies to a rack and immediately sprinkle a strainer filled with confectioners' sugar over them. If sugar melts into cookies, sprinkle with more sugar. Cookies will keep in an airtight container 2 weeks.

Makes 4 dozen cookies

Coconut–Chocolate Chip Macaroons

A very simple and elegant macaroon anyone can make. They're especially nice for the holidays as they resemble miniature snowballs.

2 large egg whites
½ cup sugar
2 tablespoons all-purpose flour
pinch of salt
½ teaspoon pure vanilla extract

½ teaspoon pure almond extract
2½ cups sweetened flaked coconut, fluffed with a fork
¼ cup mini semisweet chocolate chips

Heat oven to 325°F. Line 2 baking sheets with parchment paper or lightly buttered foil.

Beat whites till stiff peaks form. Gradually add sugar in a stream while beating. Beat in flour, salt, and extracts. Fold in coconut and chips by hand.

Wet your hands and roll coconut mixture into small rounds (about the size of golf balls). Arrange on prepared baking sheets about 1 inch apart. Bake 20 to 22 minutes, or until lightly browned. Cool on baking sheets 10 minutes before transferring to a serving plate.

Makes about 18 cookies

Becca's Almond Macaroons

These may be the best cookies I've ever eaten—they are chewy and buttery and have a wonderful almond flavor. The recipe comes from my friend Rebecca, another horse girl who owns an American saddlebred and also works as an editor for magazines. She's a great cook but comes by it honestly. Her mother, the late Jane Redd Benton, was a renowned cook from Signal Mountain, Tennessee. Becca was given this recipe from an old friend. It's definitely worth passing on.

¾ cup unsalted butter, melted

1½ cups sugar, plus more for
sprinkling

2 large eggs

1½ cups all-purpose flour

pinch of salt

1 teaspoon almond extract

½ cup sliced almonds

Preheat oven to 350°F. Line a 10-inch iron skillet with heavy-duty foil, leaving a 3-inch overhang for lifting the cookies out.

Combine the butter and next 5 ingredients (through extract) in a medium bowl, stirring with a wooden spoon. Spread the batter evenly (it will be very thick) on the bottom of the skillet. Scatter the almonds over the top and sprinkle with about 2 teaspoons of sugar.

Bake for 30 minutes or until lightly browned. Remove from oven and let stand in skillet 5 minutes. Lift the cookies out by grabbing the foil on both sides. Place on a cutting board. While still warm, cut into wedges or use a small biscuit cutter (about 2½ inches wide) or heart-shaped cutter to cut out cookies. Cookies will keep in an airtight container about 5 days.

Makes 8 to 10 cookies

Chocolate Chip Meringues

·······························

Meringues are elegant and easy cookies and so delicious when they're freshly made. I like to make these for gifts, wrap in a cellophane bag and tie with a pretty chocolate-colored ribbon.

3 large egg whites
⅛ teaspoon cream of tartar
½ teaspoon raspberry liqueur or
   vanilla extract
⅔ cup granulated sugar

1 tablespoon unsweetened cocoa
   powder
⅓ cup semisweet mini chocolate
   chips

Preheat oven to 400°F. Line 2 baking sheets with aluminum foil.

In a medium bowl, combine egg whites, cream of tartar, and raspberry liqueur. Beat with an electric mixer until stiff peaks form. Continue beating, gradually adding sugar until whites are stiff and glossy.

Sift cocoa over meringue and beat until just combined. Fold in the chips with a spatula. Drop heaping tablespoons of meringue onto baking sheets. Or place the meringue in a reclosable plastic bag. Snip off a corner and "pipe" cookies into a desired shape (a large chocolate kiss shape works nicely).

Bake 30 minutes, then turn oven off and leave meringues in the oven 1 hour or overnight.

Makes 2 dozen

Butter Pecan Cookies

This is a really great cookie from Emma with an excellent buttery pecan flavor. Toasting the chopped nuts in the butter makes all the difference.

1¾ cups finely chopped pecans

1 cup plus 1 tablespoon (2 sticks) unsalted butter, softened

1 cup packed light brown sugar

1 large egg

1 teaspoon vanilla extract

2 cups all-purpose flour

½ teaspoon salt

1 large egg white, beaten

1 cup pecan halves

Preheat oven to 325°F. Combine the chopped pecans and 1 tablespoon butter on a large baking sheet. Toast in the oven, stirring occasionally, about 7 minutes. Remove from oven and cool.

Cream the remaining butter and brown sugar until light and fluffy with an electric mixer. Beat in egg and vanilla. Stir flour and salt together. Gradually add to butter mixture until just blended. Cover bowl with plastic wrap and refrigerate at least 1 hour.

Preheat oven to 375°F. Line 2 large baking sheets with parchment or foil. Roll dough into 1-inch balls, then roll in toasted pecans, pressing nuts lightly into dough. Arrange on baking sheets about 2 inches apart. Dip underside of pecan halves into egg white and lightly press onto tops of cookies. Bake about 10 minutes, until cookies are firm and just turning golden around edges. Cool on baking sheets 2 minutes then transfer to racks to cool completely. Cookies will keep in an airtight container about 2 weeks.

Makes 4 dozen cookies

Chocolate-Covered Cherryettes

This is the cookie version of a chocolate-covered cherry that Emma always makes during the holidays. It's one of my ultimate favorites. You can top them with either semisweet or milk chocolate, depending on your preference.

2½ cups all-purpose flour

¾ cup confectioners' sugar

½ teaspoon salt

1 cup (2 sticks) unsalted butter, softened

1 teaspoon vanilla extract

½ teaspoon almond extract

¾ cup chopped candied cherries

¼ cup chopped walnuts, lightly toasted

1 cup milk or semisweet chocolate morsels, melted

Preheat oven to 350°F. Combine first 6 ingredients (through almond extract) in a large mixing bowl. Stir with a rubber spatula until just blended. Fold in cherries and walnuts.

Roll dough into 1½ inch-size balls and place on a baking sheet lined with parchment or foil. Bake 15 to 18 minutes until firm and lightly browned on bottoms. Transfer to racks until cool. Drop teaspoonfuls of chocolate over tops of cookies. Leave on racks until chocolate is firm. (Cookies freeze well.)

Makes about 4 dozen cookies

Emma's Molasses Crinkles

Have I mentioned Emma taught cookie making for years? These simple ginger snaps, which she's made since we were children, are her hallmark. They're the finest ginger cookies I've ever tried.

2½ cups all-purpose flour

2 teaspoons baking soda

3 teaspoons ground ginger

½ teaspoon ground cloves

¼ teaspoon salt

¾ cup unsalted butter, softened

¾ cup packed light brown sugar

1 large egg

¼ cup mild molasses

granulated sugar for rolling cookies

Sift together the first 5 ingredients (through salt). Cream the butter and sugar with an electric mixture until light and creamy. Add the egg and molasses and blend well. Gradually add the dry ingredients to the butter mixture, mixing until just blended. Cover and refrigerate at least 1 hour.

Preheat oven to 350°F. Line 2 backing sheets with parchment or foil. Roll cookies into 1-inch balls. Dip tops in granulated sugar and place on baking sheets, 2 inches apart. Bake 9 to 10 minutes. Cool on baking sheet 1 minute, then transfer to racks to cool completely. Cookies will keep in an airtight container 2 weeks.

Makes 4 dozen cookies

Sister's Big Buttermilk Sugar Cookies

This is my sister, Linda Combs's, contribution to the family recipe archives and it is a great one. Linda doesn't bake all that often, but she dearly loves to eat other people's cooking. These are big Amish-style sugar cookies. They're tender and cakey—just the thing to enjoy with a nice cup of hot cider. Top them with sugar or frosting. I have no idea how long they keep as they go so fast. I like to add maraschino cherry juice to the icing for a pretty pink cookie.

2 cups sugar

1 cup (2 sticks) unsalted butter, softened

3 large eggs, beaten

½ teaspoon lemon or almond extract

1 teaspoon vanilla extract

4½ cups all-purpose flour

½ teaspoon salt

5 teaspoons baking powder

1 cup buttermilk

granulated sugar (optional)

Lemon Cookie Icing (recipe follows)

Preheat oven to 375°F. Line 2 baking sheets with parchment or foil.

In a large mixing bowl with an electric mixer, beat the sugar, butter, eggs, and extracts until well blended. Stir together the flour, salt, and baking powder. Add to butter mixture alternately with the buttermilk. Drop by heaping teaspoonfuls onto baking sheets, 3 inches apart (cookies will spread quite a bit). Sprinkle with sugar or leave plain if frosting. Bake 12 to 15 minutes until cookies have risen and are golden around edges.

Cool on baking sheets 2 minutes. Transfer to racks. If desired, top with Lemon Cookie Icing while still warm. Cool completely before storing in an airtight container. Cookies will keep for about 1 week.

Makes about 3 dozen large cookies

Lemon Cookie Icing

You can also make this with orange juice and zest.

2 tablespoons unsalted butter,
softened
1 cup confectioners' sugar

1 tablespoon fresh lemon juice
2 teaspoons grated lemon zest

Whisk together the ingredients in a bowl until smooth. Apply to hot cookies with a knife.

Makes about 1/2 cup

My sister Linda and I were probably in the
midst of a scrap when our naughty Uncle
Buddy asked us to mug for the camera.

Germaine's Mint Brownies

These are pretty killer brownies from my Kentucky friend Germaine Johnson. If you're not a chocolate-mint person (usually I'm not, but these are special) you can leave out the middle layer. The brownies are chewy and gooey, just the thing to take to a potluck. They also make a good base for a hot fudge and brownie sundae (my fave).

½ cup unsalted butter, softened

½ teaspoon salt

1 cup sugar

1 (16-ounce) can Hershey syrup

4 large eggs

1 teaspoon vanilla extract

1 cup all-purpose flour

Mint Layer (recipe follows)

Fudge Frosting (recipe follows)

Preheat oven to 350°F. Butter a 9 × 13 × 2-inch pan. Cream the butter and sugar until fluffy, about 3 minutes. Add eggs, one at a time, beating after each addition. Combine the flour and salt then add to butter mixture alternating with chocolate syrup. Pour batter into prepared pan and bake for 25 to 30 minutes, until edges pull away from sides of pan. Cool completely in pan. Top with Mint Layer, then Fudge Frosting (recipes follow). Cut into 12 or 16 brownies.

Mint Layer

4 tablespoons unsalted butter, softened

2 tablespoons crème de menthe

2 cups confectioners' sugar

Cream the butter with the crème de menthe and sugar. Add more crème de menthe, a drop at a time, if mixture is stiff (it needs to be spreadable). Spread over cooled brownies and chill for at least 1 hour. Top with frosting.

Makes 12 to 16 brownies

Fudge Frosting

1 (6-ounce) package semi-sweet chocolate chips

4 tablespoons unsalted butter

Melt the chips and butter together in a microwave for 1 to 2 minutes (or in the top of double boiler). Spread over mint layer. Chill for at least 1 hour.

The black stove, stoked with coal and firewood, glows like a lighted pumpkin. Eggbeaters whirl, spoons spin round in bowls of butter and sugar, vanilla sweetens the air, ginger spices it; melting, nose-tingling odors saturate the kitchen, suffuse the house, drift out to the world on puffs of chimney smoke. In four days our work is done. Thirty-one cakes, dampened with whiskey, bask on window sills and shelves.

—Truman Capote, "A Christmas Memory"

Butterscotch-Banana Blondies

If you're like me, you prefer brownies to blondies, but these—moist from the banana, with a great butterscotch flavor—are very special.

4 tablespoons unsalted butter, plus
   more for buttering pan
1 cup packed dark brown sugar
1 large egg
1 teaspoon vanilla extract

1 cup mashed ripe banana
   (about 2 large bananas)
¼ teaspoon salt
1⅓ cups all-purpose flour
1 cup chopped pecans, toasted

Heat oven to 350°F. Line the bottom of an 8-inch square pan with waxed paper and butter the bottom and sides.

Melt the butter over low heat in a medium saucepan and add the sugar. Bring to a simmer and cook about 1 minute to dissolve the sugar. Remove from heat and cool 10 minutes. Beat in the egg, vanilla, and the banana. Stir together the salt and flour and stir into batter until just blended; fold in the nuts. Pour into the prepared pan.

Bake 35 minutes, or until blondies just pull away from the sides of the pan. Set the pan aside to cool on a rack until cool enough to handle. Invert on a rack, peel off waxed paper, turn right side up and cool completely. Place on a cutting board and use a sharp knife to cut into squares.

Makes sixteen 2-inch squares

Blu Baugh Bakery Hermits

Emma Mae around age nineteen in her Sunday best.

My mom's first job was at the phone company in Charleston. On her breaks she loved to go to the Blu Baugh Bakery on nearby Capital Street for a slice of their famous rum cake or these chewy molasses spice cookies. The bakery even had a delivery route in town (gosh, those were the days). Every time I take a bite I fantasize about quitting my day job and opening up a business just selling these. Technically, this is not the bakery's recipe but Emma claims this is the closest to her memory of them. These are baked and then sliced like a Fig Newton, but you can also spread the dough in a 9 × 13-inch pan and cut them into bars instead.

1½ cups all-purpose flour

½ cup pitted dates, chopped

⅔ cup chopped walnuts or pecans

⅓ cup packed dark brown sugar

1 teaspoon ground cinnamon

½ teaspoon freshly grated nutmeg

1 teaspoon ground ginger

½ teaspoon baking powder

¼ teaspoon salt

¼ cup robust molasses

4 tablespoons unsalted butter, melted

1 large egg, beaten

Preheat oven to 375°F. Line a large baking sheet with aluminum foil and lightly coat with cooking oil spray.

In a large bowl with a wooden spoon, stir together the first 9 ingredients (through salt). Stir in the molasses, butter, and egg until just blended. Chill dough in freezer 10 minutes. Divide dough in two. Roll each into 12-inch-long logs.

Place the rolls on the baking sheet about 3 inches apart. Pat rolls into oblong strips, about 2 inches wide. Bake 10 minutes. Remove from oven and let cool on pan 1 minute.

While hot, use a serrated knife to cut cookies crosswise into 2-inch-wide bars. Transfer with a spatula to wire racks to cool. Cookies will keep in an airtight container about 2 weeks.

Makes about 12 bars

Peanut Butter Shortbread

These fine-textured cookies are barely sweet and delicately flavored with peanuts. They're wonderful with tea.

1½ cups all-purpose flour
¼ teaspoon salt
10 tablespoons unsalted butter, softened

⅓ cup packed light brown sugar
⅓ cup crunchy peanut butter

Heat oven to 300°F. Sift together flour and salt and set aside.

Beat the butter and sugar with an electric mixer until very light and fluffy, about 3 minutes. Beat in the peanut butter until well blended. Fold in the flour mixture by hand until it's just absorbed (overmixing will cause the dough to toughen). Transfer the dough to a lightly buttered 9-inch round cake pan. Lightly flour your hands and press the dough into the prepared pan. Prick all over the top with the tines of a fork or a wooden skewer. Score the top lightly to create 8 even wedges.

Bake 30 to 35 minutes, or until lightly browned around edges. Cool on rack 5 minutes. Slice in wedges while still warm; leave shortbread in pan on a rack to cool completely. When cool, transfer to a serving plate. Will keep in an airtight container 2 weeks.

Makes 8 large cookies

Crispy Treats

My mother used to make up a pan of these marshmallow-cereal bars at night for us and place it in the freezer to firm up fast before slicing into squares. I still crave them, and it makes me smile to see these big oversize blocks in bakery windows all over New York City.

5 tablespoons unsalted butter

2 (10-ounce) packages mini marshmallows

1/2 teaspoon salt

1/2 teaspoon vanilla extract

8 cups crisp rice cereal

1 1/2 cups mini chocolate chips or mini M&Ms, optional

Butter an 8-inch square pan (or 9 × 13 for thinner treats). Melt the butter in a large, heavy-bottomed saucepan over low heat. Add marshmallows and cook, stirring, until melted. Stir in salt and vanilla. Remove from heat and stir in rice cereal. Fold in candies, if using. Quickly transfer to pan. Butter hands and press cereal lightly to make the surface even. Cool completely. Cut into 9 (or 12 if using bigger pan) even squares.

Makes 9 to 12 squares

Chocolate Turtles

These chewy chocolate, caramel, and pecan treats remind me of the candy "turtles" I used to watch being made at a downtown department store in Charleston. Working behind a glass-shielded counter, the ladies wore pink dresses with crisp white collars and paper hats on their beehives—just like Lucy and Ethel on the candy assembly line. It was mesmerizing. The candy got its name from its turtle-like shape—the nuts at the base look like stubby legs beneath the caramel mound and chocolate coating.

melted butter for brushing	6 ounces semisweet chocolate chips
100 pecan halves	4 teaspoons vegetable shortening
25 caramel candy squares	

Preheat oven to 350°F. Line 2 baking sheets with aluminum foil and brush with butter.

To make each turtle: Arrange 4 pecan halves in a cross shape on baking sheet. Place a caramel in the center of the nuts. Repeat with remaining nuts and caramels. Place in oven 5 minutes until caramel is barely melted. Remove from oven. Gently press caramel into nuts and smooth rough edges to make it more of a mound shape. Place in fridge until completely cool.

In a small glass bowl, melt the chocolate and shortening in a microwave 1 minute. Remove and stir until completely melted (return to microwave, if necessary).

Spoon a small amount of chocolate over nuts and caramels. Refrigerate until chocolate sets. Remove with a spatula and place in an airtight container lined with waxed paper between layers. Turtles will stay fresh in a cool place 5 days.

Makes 25 turtles

Lady Food: Luncheon Dishes from the Cake Club

Asparagus Canapés

Wilted Lettuce Salad

Tomato Aspic

Pickled Shrimp

Mary Cannon's Hot Water Corn Cakes

Blue Cheese Grapes

String Beans with Feta Cheese
    and Bacon

Chicken Paprikash

Divine Chicken Divan

Lady Food

What *is* Lady Food, you may ask? Lady Food is really good food, but it's wise to eat it in moderation. Oftentimes it starts with a box of Jell-O or a can of cream of mushroom soup, contains at least one teaspoon of curry powder, and is more often than not topped with a crust of purchased crunchy fried onions. Recipes with "Deluxe," "Supreme," and "Heavenly" in the title are, generally speaking, Lady Food. *Southern Living* recipes, most definitely, are Lady Food (except for the barbecue and ribs). And Junior League cookbooks are chock-full of LF. Tomatoes stuffed with chicken salad, avocados filled with crabmeat, and chicken divan are the epitome of Lady Food. Men—straight meat-and-potatoes men, that is—don't care much for Lady Food, though we ladies think it's just dandy. Eat too much of it, though, and you will become a fat lady.

The following recipes are some of the dishes the Cake Club ladies enjoyed: appetizers, salads, and a few main courses. I chose not to include selections from the dismal period when the Cake Club all decided to go on the Weight Watchers diet and filled themselves with cabbage tomato soup, French bread pizza, and the like. Miraculously, my sister, Linda, and I were never sick enough to stay home during the entire duration of the diet.

Asparagus Canapés

I have a suspicion the ladies of the Cake Club probably used canned asparagus to make this favorite. My version is a wee bit healthier, using fresh spears and sans the mayonnaise—however, white bread is a must. The canapés are quite nice—buttery asparagus with melted cheese wrapped in crusty bread. Serve as a snack with lots of napkins.

12 slices good-quality soft white bread, crusts trimmed

¾ cup grated Gruyère or Swiss cheese

12 asparagus spears, cooked tender

4 tablespoons unsalted butter, melted

Preheat oven to 400°F. Arrange the bread on a counter and flatten ever so slightly with a rolling pin, but don't mash out the air. (This will keep the bread from breaking apart.)

Divide the cheese between the bread slices and place on one half of bread to edge. Place an asparagus spear at the edge of the cheese side. Trim the asparagus ends to the length of the bread and roll them up like crepes.

Brush the rolls lightly with the butter and place folded side down on a baking sheet lined with parchment paper or foil to secure it (use a toothpick if they try to unroll). Bake 10 to 12 minutes until browned and crisp. Let cool slightly before serving.

Serves 12 as an appetizer

Wilted Lettuce Salad

After I left home I was surprised that few people outside of Appalachia knew of this salad (after all, why would you want to eat wilted *lettuce?). But it's quite wonderful, and even better if you start with a crisp head of leaf lettuce from a farmer's market. In our house a small amount of hot bacon drippings were used to cook and flavor garden vegetables like cabbage, dandelion greens, and spinach. For this recipe, I grew up with, I added some olive oil to make the dressing a bit lighter in consistency and flavor. The salad can be made with all sorts of greens; watercress, dandelion greens, and arugula are especially nice mixed with the lettuce. Assemble all the ingredients ahead of time and toss just before you're ready to serve. Be sure to grind extra pepper over the top.*

4 pieces bacon, fried crisp, drippings reserved

1 large head leaf lettuce, torn into medium-size pieces

4 scallions, coarsely chopped, white and dark green parts separated

2 tablespoons extra-virgin olive oil

2 tablespoons apple cider vinegar

1 tablespoon sugar

pinch each of salt and freshly ground black pepper

2 large hard-cooked eggs, peeled and chopped (optional)

Cook the bacon and reserve the drippings. Combine the lettuce and green tops of the scallions in a large salad bowl.

Heat 2 tablespoons of the bacon drippings, olive oil, vinegar, sugar, salt, and pepper in a medium pan over medium-high flame. Stir to dissolve sugar and bring to a simmer. Add white parts of scallions and stir-fry about 30 seconds.

Pour a little of the hot dressing over the greens and toss to coat the greens (add only enough to lightly coat). Add more salt and pepper, if desired. Crumble bacon and top with eggs, if using. Serve warm.

Serves 4 to 6

Tomato Aspic

The cake ladies loved their molded "salads," all of which started with an envelope or two of Knox gelatin. I can appreciate a well-made Jell-O salad and particularly like this classic tomato aspic. My friend Ouita Michel, who owns the Holly Hill Inn in Midway, Kentucky, which she runs with her husband, Chris, has a brilliant idea for serving this dish. She adds enough horseradish to make the aspic spicy, like cocktail sauce. Then she pours it into individual martini glasses to set. Before serving, she hangs the shrimp on the rim of the glass for an elegant twist on a shrimp cocktail. Other nice variations include adding a cup of finely diced fennel, celery, or cucumber. It is especially wonderful made with homemade or organic tomato juice. Serve thin slices of aspic on butter lettuce leaves with a small spoonful of Duke's mayonnaise (a southern specialty) on top. Serve the Pickled Shrimp (recipe follows) on the side. This is bona fide Lady Food.

5 cups tomato juice	White Wine Worcestershire
3 envelopes unflavored gelatin	sauce to taste
1 garlic clove, crushed	hot sauce to taste
¼ cup fresh lemon juice	prepared horseradish to taste
2 teaspoons to 1 tablespoon sugar	(optional)

Place 1 cup tomato juice in a large bowl. Sprinkle gelatin over juice and blend with a whisk. Place 2 cups tomato juice and crushed garlic in a small saucepan and bring to a boil. Remove from heat and whisk into gelatin mixture. Stir in remaining 2 cups tomato juice, lemon juice, and add sugar, Worcestershire sauce, and hot sauce to taste. Add horseradish, if using.

Pour into a 5½-cup ring mold or bowl (or individual 1-cup Pyrex dishes or martini glasses). Chill until firm, about 4 hours or overnight. To serve, dip mold or bowls briefly in a bowl of hot water and run a butter knife around the edge to release; invert onto a plate (if using martini glasses just leave aspic in it to serve). Slice and serve over lettuce leaves with a dollop of mayonnaise.

Serves 6 to 12

Pickled Shrimp

Pickling is a simple way to cook shrimp in the shell. The result is delicious warm or chilled and nice to take on a picnic. For shrimp cocktails, peel before serving.

5 cups dry white wine

5 cups water

1 small lemon, quartered

2 fresh bay leaves (or dried will do)

8 black peppercorns

1 tablespoon kosher salt

2 pounds fresh or frozen medium or
large shrimp, shells on

Combine first 6 ingredients (through salt) in a large saucepan and bring to a boil. Boil 10 minutes. Strain and return liquid to pan and bring to a boil Add shrimp and boil just 1 to 2 minutes, until they turn bright pink. Drain and cool. Serve warm or chilled.

Serves 4 to 6

Mary Cannon's Hot Water Corn Cakes

Mary Cannon was the longtime housekeeper of Minnie Pearl (whose real name was Sarah Cannon, though the two were not related). Both Mary and Minnie were incredible cooks and loved to eat. There was always something happening in the kitchen—either on or in the stove—breakfast, lunch, or dinner. Mary's corn cakes were made just about daily and she would often wrap a couple up for me to take home. I'd never tasted these before I moved to Nashville, where a cook is judged by how well they can make them. Mary's are ultracrusty and the cornmeal inside is moist and plump. (They are best made with the bacon drippings, of course.) All the ladies I know in Nashville would order the "diet plates" at the luncheon hot spots like the Belle Meade Country Club or Satsuma Tea House, just so they could enjoy their corn cakes and butter. These are good as a side dish with the Wilted Lettuce Salad or the Tomato Aspic and Pickled Shrimp, or 'most anything else you'd care to eat. Actually, they're pretty good all by themselves.

2 cups white cornmeal

1 teaspoon salt

½ teaspoon baking soda

1 teaspoon baking powder

1½ cups boiling water

6 tablespoons bacon drippings or
   vegetable oil

Preheat oven to 400°F. Place 3 tablespoons of bacon drippings or oil in a large iron skillet and place in the oven to heat. (You can also leave on the stove and heat over medium flame.)

Stir the cornmeal, salt, baking soda, and baking powder together. While stirring with a fork, slowly add the boiling water into the dry ingredients. Stir in the remaining drippings and blend until everything is well moistened. When cool enough to handle, form large egg-shaped cakes in your hands and place in the hot skillet. Bake 20 minutes (or fry on top of the stove) until golden brown. (If frying, turn once.) Serve hot with butter.

Makes 10 cakes

Blue Cheese Grapes

The ladies of the club always loved these grapes. I thought they were very sophisticated, and I still like to serve them. The sweetness of the grapes is a perfect foil for the strong flavor of the blue cheese. You can make them up to 2 days ahead and keep refrigerated in a sealed container.

1 (8-ounce) package cream cheese, softened

⅔ cup crumbled Stilton or other blue cheese

about 1 pound (around 50 or so) large seedless red or green grapes

12 ounces shelled pistachios or walnuts, finely chopped and lightly toasted

In a large bowl, cream together the cheeses with an electric mixer until smooth. If it's too thick, add a few drops of milk to make it creamy. Fold the grapes in by hand until all are coated. Refrigerate 30 minutes, until cheese mixture is slightly firm.

Place the chopped nuts on a large plate. Line a large baking sheet with waxed paper or foil. Moisten hands and remove grapes and roll in your hand to form a cheese-coated ball. Roll each ball in the nuts until coated. Transfer to the baking sheet. Cover with plastic wrap and refrigerate until firm, about 30 minutes. Transfer to a tightly sealed container until ready to serve.

Makes 50, enough for 12 servings or more

String Beans with Feta Cheese and Bacon

This recipe is based on a rather heavy casserole the ladies always served at the buffet. This lighter version uses fresh crisp beans from the garden or farmer's market, topped with a simple sauce.

3 ounces good quality feta, crumbled

⅓ cup buttermilk

1 tablespoon fresh lemon juice

½ teaspoon freshly ground black pepper

1½ pounds fresh string beans, trimmed

4 strips bacon, fried crisp, crumbled

Combine half of feta, buttermilk, lemon juice, and pepper in a blender and purée. Set aside.

Steam beans until crisp tender. Transfer to a serving platter. Drizzle dressing over beans and top with remaining cheese and crumbled bacon.

Serves 6

Tastes Like Chicken (Dining on the Wild Side in West Virginia)

Squirrels are delicious. I like the red ones best—all fat from gobbling up acorns and hickory nuts. You hardly see them anymore. My granddaddy used to hunt squirrels on the weekends, then skin and dress them in the woods. He'd bring them home all shiny and pink and if it was your turn, you got the furry tail to scare your sister with.

Some people would salt the squirrels and soak them in brine overnight to remove the gaminess. My grandmother would literally scrub them with the salt, washing them like laundry. To cook the squirrel you cut it into pieces at the joint, dipped them in egg, then dredged them in flour seasoned with salt, lots of pepper, and a little paprika. You need to fry squirrel slowly, purposefully, in hot lard until it's crispy on the outside and the juice runs clear. Then you make a gravy with a little bit of the drippings, flour, milk, and even more pepper, and serve it with hot biscuits. Squirrel tastes so good you can hardly believe it. Juicy, tender, and falling off the bone. Like chicken, only buttery from all the nuts the little hummers eat.

On the other hand, there's rabbit. *Very* tasty. A fresh rabbit—watch out for the buckshot—is best stewed in a thick gravy flavored with onion and stewed tomatoes. It's so good "you want to hit yourself," as my crazy uncle Buddy always says. You sop up the gravy with bread to get every last bit. Cheap white bread works best—the ultimate sponge. Rabbit, as a matter of fact, tastes a little like chicken, only better because it's *not*.

If it is true that you are what you eat then I am made up of many wild things that lived or grew in the mountains of Appalachia. My family, even in the late 1960s and early 1970s, still farmed, hunted, fished, and ate pretty much the way their grandparents did. They knew how to survive as they say, quite literally, off the land. They cooked with bacon grease, real lard, butter, and a little cream on top. They ate pie and cake after almost every meal, and no one was fat because they worked hard all the livelong day. Their water came from a spring or a well. They knew the trees that bore nuts, what berries were good to eat, and where a copperhead might be lurking. They could divine a spring with a three-pronged branch and sniff out a sassafras tree a mile away.

They knew about pawpaws. Have you ever seen a pawpaw tree? They hang heavy from branches in the fall and are good only after they've sat a few days nestled on the ground, turned black as coal, and squishy as a ripe banana. You can mash the pulp and make a sweet bread or turn it into a stiff pudding with cornmeal mush like the Indians did.

Dandelion greens are best when they first sprout up and you can gather them right from the yard. Add them to a salad and toss with hot bacon dressing and a little vinegar and sugar. Poke-weed greens are bitter but not bad either, if nipped young and just peeking their green tongues out of the ground.

Ramps are sort of a cross between a green onion, garlic, and a leek. Very intense at first but don't let that scare you away. Stew them in a big pot with a mess of greens—creasy are my favorite (wild cress you find by a creek), followed by turnip and mustard. You spoon the greens and ramps in a bowl with the cooking juices and crumble cornbread over it to soak up the broth. That's pot likker, to you and me. Filled with vitamins, it's a good tonic for the body after a long winter of eating nothing but canned vegetables.

Something to remember (if you ever get lost in the woods and need to survive for real), is that hickory nuts can be hard as marble. You need a hammer to crack them open and this is best accomplished in the crevice of a rock. Hickory nuts make the best cakes but it takes an entire day to get enough of the nutmeat for even a small loaf. You can have all the black walnuts though, for I never could stand them.

Tea from a sassafras tree is pinkish red and tastes faintly of licorice but I think it is what tea must taste like in heaven (especially with honey). They say it causes cancer—truly, it is banned by the FDA—but my aunt Martha drank it every day of her life and lived to be 110 and with her mind intact, so maybe it's actually a *preservative*. We still make it for special occasions as it reminds us of her and where we came from. I once made a sassafras tea sorbet for a dinner party and my fancy food friends swore they'd risk liver disease to have it again. It's that good.

I love the foods I grew up with, though I did not always. There were whole years where I did not eat a bowl of beans or a slice of cornbread, or even think much about it. When I was a novice food writer working at a fancy magazine, I went to Tuscany with a bunch of other, much more important food writers. Among other things, we ate hot, creamy polenta (grits); big bowls of brown bean soup with hog cheeks (née jowls); tender cooked kale served over garlic toast (pot likker); and beans and rice with pancetta mixed in it (hoppin' John!). We ate more pork in Tuscany than you could shake a pig at. There were also lots of rabbit and other game dishes on the menus, salads of dandelion greens, and all sorts of vegetables and grains flavored with smoked bacon bits and pan drippings. It all tasted so *familiar*. The food was simply made, as it had been for centuries, and it wasn't just the working class who were eating this way but elegant ladies wearing Gucci and Armani who sipped Chianti with their earthy dinners. I was so struck by the similarity to the food our family grew and ate that I felt an immediate connection and a twinkle of pride.

When I got back home I thought of my Italian friends who visited New York and inevitably asked, "Just what *is* American cuisine?" Or, "Is there a national dish . . . *besides* hamburgers?" If only they had visited West Virginia, where I come from. There they would have tasted a part of the story of American food. I think they would have liked the fried squirrel in particular.

Chicken Paprikash

The recipe for this classic dish is pretty heavy for modern tastes. I use chicken breasts and only a bit of sour cream and it's just as rich and satisfying. I prefer the flavor of smoky Spanish paprika for a change of pace, but Hungarian is good, too. Just make sure your spice is fairly new. Fresh bay leaves add a touch of oomph. Serve it over hot egg noodles tossed with a bit of butter and chopped fresh parsley.

6 boneless, skinless, chicken breast
  halves
salt and freshly ground black pepper
  to taste
4 teaspoons olive oil
1 medium onion, thinly sliced
¼ cup sweet Spanish (or Hungarian)
  paprika

2 tablespoons all-purpose flour
1½ cups homemade or low-sodium
  chicken stock
1 garlic clove, minced
1 fresh or dried bay leaf
¾ cup sour cream
1 tablespoon butter

Place chicken breasts between 2 sheets of plastic wrap. Using a rolling pin or mallet, pound the chicken to ½-inch thickness. Season both sides with salt and pepper.

Heat 2 teaspoons of the oil in a large nonstick skillet over medium-high heat. Brown chicken, in batches, on both sides, 2 to 4 minutes, or until just cooked through. Add more oil, as needed. Transfer to a plate and keep warm.

Reduce heat to medium and add onions to skillet. Cook, stirring, until onions are soft and golden brown, about 5 to 7 minutes. Add paprika and flour to skillet and stir to coat. Add the broth, garlic, and bay leaf. Bring to a simmer, stirring frequently, and cook 10 minutes.

Return the chicken and any accumulated juices to the skillet (you can slice the chicken first, if you wish); bring to a simmer. Cover and cook 5 minutes, or just until heated through. Stir in the sour cream and butter until well blended and season to taste with salt and pepper. Bring to a simmer and remove from heat. Serve over hot noodles or rice.

Serves 4 to 6

Divine Chicken Divan

This was a favorite casserole of the Cake Clubbers (and yes, oftentimes they used canned cream of mushroom soup rather than making a white sauce). You can also add a teaspoon of curry powder to the sauce but I prefer it as is. It's also good made ahead of time and refrigerated. Bring to room temperature before topping with the last of the cheese and almonds and broiling as directed.

2 cups homemade chicken broth or
    low-sodium canned broth
4 boneless skinless chicken breast
    halves (about 1½ pounds total)
1½ bunches broccoli, trimmed and cut
    into long spears
½ stick (¼ cup) unsalted butter, cut
    into pieces

1 small onion, thinly sliced
1½ cups thinly sliced mushrooms
4 tablespoons all-purpose flour
¼ cup heavy cream
3 tablespoons dry sherry
½ cup freshly grated Parmesan
¼ cup sliced almonds

Bring the chicken broth to a boil in a medium saucepan and add the chicken breasts. Lower heat and simmer until chicken is just cooked through, about 8 minutes. Remove from broth and let sit 5 minutes before thinly slicing crosswise. Cover with foil and keep warm. Strain the broth and reserve it for making the sauce.

In a large saucepan of boiling salted water cook the broccoli until just tender, about 5 minutes. Drain. Butter a 9 × 13 × 2-inch glass baking dish and arrange broccoli spears across the bottom. Cover with foil and keepwarm.

In a heavy saucepan melt the butter over medium heat and sauté the onions until they are soft. Add the mushrooms and cook until tender and browned. Add the flour and cook, stirring, for 3 minutes. Stir in the broth and bring to a boil; reduce heat to low and simmer 5 minutes until thickened. Add the chicken and simmer 1 minute. Stir in the cream, sherry, and half the Parmesan into the sauce and simmer 2 minutes. Remove from heat and season to taste with salt and freshly ground black pepper.

Preheat the broiler to high and arrange a rack 6 inches below the heat source. Pour the chicken and sauce over the broccoli in the baking dish. Top with the remaining ¼ cup Parmesan and the almonds. Broil the mixture (watch carefully) for 1 minute until it bubbles and the topping is golden brown.

Serves 6

Index

· · · · · · · · · · · · · · ·

Index
· · · · · · · · ·

Index
. . . .

Index
· · · · · · · · ·